# BLUEPRINT
## Infant
## Topic Planner

# Stanley Thornes (Publishers) Ltd

## Do you receive *BLUEPRINTS NEWS*?

Blueprints is an expanding series of practical teacher's ideas books and photocopiable resources for use in primary schools. Books are available for separate infant and junior age ranges for every core and foundation subject, as well as for an ever widening range of other primary teaching needs. These include **Blueprints Primary English** books and **Blueprints Resource Banks**. **Blueprints** are carefully structured around the demands of National Curriculum in England and Wales, but are used successfully by schools and teachers in Scotland, Northern Ireland and elsewhere.

**Blueprints** provide:

- Total curriculum coverage
- Hundreds of practical ideas
- Books specifically for the age range you teach
- Flexible resources for the whole school or for individual teachers
- Excellent photocopiable sheets – ideal for assessment and children's work profiles
- Supreme value.

Books may be bought by credit card over the telephone and information obtained on **(01242) 577944**. Alternatively, photocopy and return this **FREEPOST** form to receive **Blueprints News**, our regular update on all new and existing titles. You may also like to add the name of a friend who would be interested in being on the mailing list.

---

Please add my name to the **BLUEPRINTS NEWS** mailing list.

Mr/Mrs/Miss/Ms _____

Home address _____

_____ Postcode _____

School address _____

_____ Postcode _____

Please also send **BLUEPRINTS NEWS** to:

Mr/Mrs/Miss/Ms _____

Address _____

_____ Postcode _____

To: Marketing Services Dept., Stanley Thornes Ltd, FREEPOST (GR 782), Cheltenham, GL50 1BR

---

First published in 1996 by:
Stanley Thornes (Publishers) Ltd
Ellenborough House
Wellington Street
CHELTENHAM GL50 1YW

A catalogue record for this book is available from the British Library.

ISBN 0–7487–1748–X

Typeset by Tech Set Limited, Gateshead, Tyne & Wear
Printed in Great Britain at Redwood Books Ltd.,
Trowbridge, Wiltshire.

96 97 98 99 00 / 10 9 8 7 6 5 4 3 2

# CONTENTS

# INTRODUCTION

The aim of the Blueprints Topic Planners is to provide you with the resources to plan and deliver carefully structured topic work. They have been written in response to the demands of many Blueprints users for help in delivering properly planned and focused topic work with clear learning objectives and coherent activities, rather than the more random 'cross-curricular' topics which used to be popular in primary schools in the past.

For this reason, this Topic Planner is structured closely around the programmes of study for Key Stage 1 National Curriculum to enable you to provide coherent coverage of the National Curriculum in your topic work. Each topic focuses on the curriculum content of a few subjects in detail, with supporting ideas for the rest, rather than providing an even spread of ideas across the whole curriculum. Schools not following National Curriculum work will also find the structure of the ideas valuable for their own topic work.

This book covers 23 core infant topics. Nearly all the common topics widely used in infant classes to deliver the curriculum will be found in this book. A few unusual topics have also been added, to provide occasional opportunities for variety and novelty.

For each topic we have provided:

● A topic web overviewing the curriculum coverage of the topic. Key curriculum areas are shaded.

● Starting points to get the topic going.
● A bank of outline ideas for each curriculum area, linked to coverage of the programme of study which is cross-referenced to the publication *Key Stages 1 and 2 of the National Curriculum* (HMSO, 1995) by letter and number.
● Blueprints links: an index explaining where else to go in the Blueprints series to find ideas and copymasters linked to the topic.

At the front of the book you will find a matrix overviewing the coverage of the topics. This enables you to see at a glance which parts of the National Currriculum programme of study each topic covers.

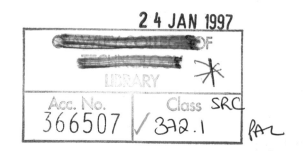

# NATIONAL CURRICULUM COVERAGE

This chart shows curriculum areas and programme of study coverage for each topic

● = substantial coverage
○ = some coverage

| | ENGLISH | | | MATHS | | | SCIENCE | | | | D&T | GEOGRAPHY | | | | | |
|---|---|---|---|---|---|---|---|---|---|---|---|---|---|---|---|---|---|
| | Speaking & listening | Reading | Writing | Using & applying maths | Number | Shape, space & measures | Experimental & investigative science | Life processes & living things | Materials & their properties | Physical processes | Designing & making skills | Skills | Places | Themes | HISTORY | ART | MUSIC |
| Ourselves | ● | ○ | ● | | ○ | ○ | ○ | ● | | | | ○ | ○ | ○ | ○ | ○ | |
| Homes | ○ | ○ | ○ | | ○ | ○ | | | ● | ○ | ○ | ○ | ○ | ○ | ● | ● | |
| Colour | ● | ○ | ○ | ○ | ● | ● | ● | ○ | ○ | | ○ | ○ | ○ | | ○ | ● | ● |
| Transport | ○ | ○ | ○ | ○ | ● | ○ | ● | | | ○ | ○ | ● | ● | ● | ● | ○ | ○ |
| Seasons | ○ | ○ | ● | ○ | ○ | | ● | ● | | ○ | | ○ | ○ | | | ● | ○ |
| Farms | ○ | ○ | ● | ○ | ○ | ○ | ● | ● | | | | ● | ● | ● | ○ | ● | |
| Toys | ○ | ○ | ○ | ● | | ○ | ○ | | ○ | | ○ | | | | ○ | ○ | |
| Shops | ○ | | ○ | ○ | ○ | ○ | ○ | ○ | ○ | | ● | ● | ● | ○ | ● | ○ | |
| Holidays | ● | ○ | ○ | ○ | ○ | ○ | ○ | ○ | ○ | ○ | ● | ○ | ○ | ○ | ○ | ○ | ○ |
| Our town | ○ | ○ | ○ | | | | ○ | ○ | ○ | | | ● | ● | ● | ● | ○ | |
| Underground | ○ | ○ | ● | | | | ○ | ● | ● | | | ● | ● | ● | | ○ | ○ |
| Pets | ● | ○ | ● | | ○ | | ○ | ○ | | | ● | | | | ○ | ● | |
| Birthdays | ○ | ○ | ○ | ○ | ○ | | ○ | ● | | | | ○ | ○ | | ● | | ○ |
| Yesterdays | ● | ○ | ● | | ○ | | ○ | ○ | ○ | ○ | | ● | ● | ● | ● | ○ | ○ |
| Trees | ● | ○ | ● | | ○ | ● | ● | ● | ● | | ○ | ● | ● | ● | | ● | |
| Minibeasts | ● | ○ | ● | | ○ | ○ | ○ | ● | | | ○ | ○ | ○ | | | ○ | |
| People | ○ | ○ | ● | | ○ | | | ● | | | ● | ● | ● | | ● | ○ | ○ |
| The Earth in space | ○ | ○ | ○ | ○ | ● | ○ | ○ | ○ | ○ | ○ | ● | ○ | ○ | | ○ | ○ | ○ |
| Climate | ○ | ○ | ○ | ○ | ○ | ● | ○ | ○ | ○ | | ○ | ○ | ○ | ○ | ○ | ● | ● |
| Rain | ● | ○ | ● | | ○ | | ● | ○ | | | ○ | ● | ● | | | ○ | ○ |
| China | ○ | ○ | ● | ○ | ○ | ○ | ○ | ○ | ○ | | ● | ● | ● | ● | ○ | ● | ○ |
| Chocolate | ○ | ○ | ○ | | ● | | ● | | ● | | ○ | ○ | ○ | | ○ | ○ | |
| Pictures | ○ | ○ | ○ | ○ | | | ○ | | ● | | ○ | ○ | ○ | | ● | ● | ○ |

● = substantial coverage
○ = some coverage

| | P.E. | R.E. | HEALTH EDUCATION | ENVIRONMENTAL EDUCATION | CITIZENSHIP | ECONOMIC & INDUSTRIAL UNDERSTANDING |
|---|---|---|---|---|---|---|
| Ourselves | ○ | ○ | | | | |
| Homes | | ● | | | | |
| Colour | | | | | | |
| Transport | | | ○ | ○ | | |
| Seasons | | ○ | | | | |
| Farms | | | | ● | | ○ |
| Toys | ○ | | | | | |
| Shops | | ○ | ○ | | | |
| Holidays | ○ | | ○ | | | |
| Our town | | | | ○ | ○ | ○ |
| Underground | | | | ○ | | |
| Pets | | ○ | ○ | | | |
| Birthdays | | ○ | | | | |
| Yesterdays | | | ○ | | | |
| Trees | | ○ | | ○ | | |
| Minibeasts | | ○ | | | | |
| People | | ○ | | | ○ | |
| The Earth in space | ○ | ○ | ○ | | | |
| Climate | ○ | | ○ | | | |
| Rain | ○ | ○ | | | | |
| China | ○ | ○ | | | | |
| Chocolate | | | ○ | | ○ | |
| Pictures | ○ | | | | | |

# BLUEPRINTS INFANT TOPIC PLANNER

**Blueprints topic index**

This index provides an overview of how the Blueprints series can provide resources to meet the needs of key infant topics. The books mentioned contain ideas and photocopiable activities for the related topics.

**Air:** Assemblies 5-8; Topics Key Stage 1; Science Key Stage 1

**Animals:** Art Key Stage 1; Art Resource Bank; History Key Stage 1; Infant Geography Resource Bank; Infant Teacher's Resource Bank; Writing 5-8; Science Key Stage 1; Poetry Book; Technology Key Stage 1; Topics 5-8; Writing Book

**Autumn:** Assemblies 5-8; Seasonal Topics

**Birds:** Art Resource Bank; Technology Key Stage 1

**Books:** Religious Education Key Stage 1

**Bonfire night:** Festivals

**Brazil:** Distant Places

**Buildings:** Infant Geography Resource Bank; Technology Key Stage 1; Second Topics Key Stage 1

**Caring:** Assemblies 5-8; Christmas Key Stage 1

**Celebrations:** Christmas Key Stage 1; Easter; History Key Stage 1: Festivals; Religious Education Key Stage 1; Writing 5-8

**Ceramics:** Art Key Stage 1

**Change:** Technology Key Stage 1

**Childhood:** History Key Stage 1

**China:** Festivals

**Christmas:** Christmas Art and Craft; Christmas Key Stage 1; Infant Teacher's Resource Bank

**Circuses:** Art Key Stage 1

**Clothes:** Assemblies 5-8; Christmas Key Stage 1; Art Key Stage 1; History Key Stage 1; Science Key Stage 1; Topics 5-8; Writing 5-8; Technology Key Stage 1

**Colour:** Assemblies 5-8, Art Key Stage 1; Topics 5-8; Science Key Stage 1; Technology Key Stage 1

**Communication:** History Key Stage 1; Writing 5-8; Science Key Stage 1; Second Topics Key Stage 1

**Consideration:** Assemblies 5-8

**Customs:** Easter

**Counting:** History Key Stage 1; Technology Key Stage 1

**Day:** Science Key Stage 1; Poetry Book

**Dinosaurs:** Topics Key Stage 1

**Distant places:** Distant Places; Infant Geography Resource Bank

**Diwali:** Festivals

**Drugs and medicines:** Health Education Key Stage 1; Science Key Stage 1

**Earth:** Science Key Stage 1; Poetry Book

**Easter:** Easter; Festivals; Infant Teacher's Resource Bank

**Eggs:** Easter

**Egypt:** Distant Places

**Energy:** Environmental Education Key Stage 1; Science Key Stage 1; Technology Key Stage 1

**Entertainment:** Writing 5-8

**Environment:** Environmental Education Key Stage 1; Geography Key Stage 1; Health Education Key Stage 1; Technology Key Stage 1

**Family:** Assemblies 5-8; Art Key Stage 1; History Key Stage 1; Topics Key Stage 1; Health Education Key Stage 1; Geography Key Stage 1; Poetry Book; Religious Education Key Stage 1; Science Key Stage 1; Writing 5-8

**Farms:** Environmental Education Key Stage 1; Infant Geography Resource Bank; Technology Key Stage 1; Second Topics Key Stage 1

**Favourite things:** Assemblies 5-8

**Feelings:** Poetry Book

**Fire:** Topics Key Stage 1

**Flight:** Technology Key Stage 1

**Flowers:** Art Resource Bank

**Food:** Assemblies 5-8; Christmas Key Stage 1; Environmental Educational Key Stage 1; History Key Stage 1; Infant Geography Resource Bank; Infant Teacher's Resource Bank; Writing 5-8; Health Education Key Stage 1; Science Key Stage 1; Second Topics Key Stage 1

**Forces:** Science Key Stage 1; Technology Key Stage 1

**Games:** Poetry Book; Technology Key Stage 1

**Greece:** Distant Places

**Growth:** Festivals; Science Key Stage 1; Religious Education Key Stage 1; Seasonal Topics

**Hallowe'en:** Festivals

**Harvest:** Festivals; Seasonal Topics

**Holidays:** History Key Stage 1; Writing 5-8

**Homes:** Art Key Stage 1; History Key Stage 1; Infant Geography Resource Bank; Second Topics Key Stage 1; Topics 5-8; Technology Key Stage 1; Science Key Stage 1; Writing 5-8

**Islam:** Festivals

**Japan:** Distant Places

**Journeys:** Infant Geography Resource Bank

**Judaism:** Festivals

**Knights and castles:** Topics 5-8

**Landscapes:** Infant Geography Resource Bank

**Life cycles:** Easter; Science Key Stage 1

**Living things:** Art Key Stage 1; Science Key Stage 1; Seasonal Topics

**Machines:** Poetry Book; Technology Key Stage 1
**Making things:** Infant Geography Resource Bank
**Maps:** Geography Key Stage 1, Infant Geography Resource Bank
**Materials:** Art Key Stage 1; Infant Geography Resource Bank; Science Key Stage 1
**May Day:** Festivals; Infant Teacher's Resource Bank; Seasonal Topics
**Me:** Religious Education Key Stage 1
**Money:** History Key Stage 1
**Mother's Day:** Assemblies 5-8
**My body:** Topics Key Stage 1; Health Education Key Stage 1; Science Key Stage 1
**Myself:** Assemblies 5-8; Art Key Stage 1; Health Education Key Stage 1; History Key Stage 1 Infant Geography Resource Bank; Topics 5-8; Writing 5-8; Science Key Stage 1; Religious Education Key Stage 1; Writing Book

**Neighbourhood:** Geography Key Stage 1; Infant Geography Resource Bank; Writing 5-8
**New Zealand:** Distant Places
**Night:** Science Key Stage 1; Poetry Book
**Nursery rhymes:** Early Years Songs and Rhymes; Infant Teacher's Resource Bank

**Oceans:** Environmental Education Key Stage 1; Poetry Book
**Ourselves:** (see myself)

**People:** Art Resource Bank; History Key Stage 1; Science Key Stage 1; Poetry Book
**People who help us:** Assemblies 5-8; Infant Geography Resource Bank; Second Topics Key Stage 1
**Pets:** Topics 5-8; Writing 5-8
**Pirates:** Topics 5-8; Technology Key Stage 1
**Places:** Art Resource Bank; Geography Key Stage 1
**Plants:** Art Resource Bank; Infant Geography Resource Bank; Infant Teacher's Resource Bank; Science Key Stage 1; Poetry Book; Technology Key Stage 1
**Ponds:** Environmental Education Key Stage 1; Infant Geography Resource Bank
**Protection:** Topics Key Stage 1

**Rivers:** Infant Geography Resource Bank

**Safety:** Health Education Key Stage 1
**School:** History Key Stage 1; Infant Geography Resource Bank; Geography Key Stage 1; Topics Key Stage 1; Technology Key Stage 1, Writing Book

**Sea:** History Key Stage 1, Poetry Book; Environmental Education Key Stage 1; Second Topics Key Stage 1
**Seasons:** Infant Geography Resource Bank; Seasonal Topics; Science Key Stage 1; Poetry Book; Assemblies 5-8; Christmas Key Stage 1; Writing 5-8; Easter
**Senses:** Poetry Book
**Shape:** Topics 5-8; Technology Key Stage 1
**Shopping:** History Key Stage 1; Infant Geography Resource Bank; Technology Key Stage 1
**Signs and signals:** Assemblies 5-8; Infant Geography Resource Bank; Technology Key Stage 1
**Sound:** Technology Key Stage 1
**Space:** Science Key Stage 1; Infant Teacher's Resource Bank; Poetry Book; Technology Key Stage 1
**Spring:** Assemblies 5-8; Seasonal Topics; Festivals; Science Key Stage 1
**Summer:** Assemblies 5-8, Seasonal Topics, Festivals, Science Key Stage 1

**Time:** Assemblies 5-8; History Key Stage 1; Writing 5-8; Technology Key Stage 1; Second Topics Key Stage 1
**Toys and games:** History Key Stage 1; Topics Key Stage 1
**Transport:** Art Key Stage 1; Art Resource Bank; History Key Stage 1; Geography Key Stage 1; Infant Geography Resource Bank; Topics 5-8; Writing 5-8; Poetry Book; Technology Key Stage 1
**Trees:** Environmental Education Key Stage 1; Infant Geography Resource Bank; Science Key Stage 1

**Underground:** Topics 5-8
**USA:** Distant Places, Festivals

**Waste:** Environmental Education Key Stage 1
**Water:** Art Key Stage 1; Environmental Education Key Stage 1; Geography Key Stage 1; Infant Geography Resource Bank; Topics 5-8; Topics Key Stage 1; Writing 5-8; Technology Key Stage 1
**Weather:** Environmental Education Key Stage 1; Geography Key Stage 1; Infant Geography Resource Bank; Topics 5-8; Poetry Book; Writing Book
**Winter:** Assemblies 5-8; Seasonal Topics, Technology Key Stage 1
**Work:** Assemblies 5-8; Environmental Education Key Stage 1; Geography Key Stage 1, Infant Geography Resource Bank; History Key Stage 1
**Writing and printing:** Art Resource Bank; Religious Education Key Stage 1

# OURSELVES

## ENGLISH

- Talk about personal identification
- Discuss individual differences
- Describe and identify others
- Communicate experiences and feelings
- Read about people and body parts
- Appreciate our need to read
- Write about ourselves and others
- Label body parts
- Write about life without a 'perfect' body
- Compose imaginary stories
- Write about fictitious creatures
- Write accurate labels for creatures in the classroom

## HEALTH EDUCATION

- Find out about keeping the body healthy
- Consider who helps to look after us

## ART

- Make portraits and profiles
- Make finger and foot prints
- Paint body parts
- Make posters about body care
- Make an 'ourselves' display

## R.E.

- Investigate racial/religious identity

## OURSELVES

## GEOGRAPHY

- Study similarities and differences between ourselves and people from distant lands

## MATHEMATICS

- Measure and compare body part size and area
- Do tooth counts
- Collect, display and interpret data on body parts and related processes
- Do eye colour surveys
- Take heart and pulse rates

## P.E.

- Consider the effects of P.E. and exercise on our bodies

## HISTORY

- Study people of the past and consider changes
- Discuss how *we* have changed through time

## SCIENCE

- Make collages of the body and its parts
- Consider the inter-connectedness of body parts
- Use body parts to perform unusual tasks
- Design fair tests of body functions
- Identify boys and girls
- Identify friends using limited features
- Consider essential life processes
- Consider which body parts are essential
- Study the human skeleton
- Find out about 'hidden' body parts
- Test for colour blindness
- Find out about inherited characteristics

1

**IDEAS BANK**
General starting points: Suggestions for programmes of study of core and foundation subjects relating to topic, and links with cross-curricular themes and R.E.

**STARTING POINTS**
● Go around the class asking children to say their full names. Point out that we are all boys and girls in the same class, but we are all 'special' and different people.
● Ask the children to bring to school a photograph of themselves and of close family members.

● Have a discussion on 'favourite foods', 'favourite games' or 'favourite places', helping children to appreciate that individuals have differing likes and dislikes.
● Ask the children to look carefully at each other – describe and discuss what makes each of us a different person, for example, hair and eye colour, size and shape, facial expression and so on.

# ENGLISH ▶

**Speaking and listening**
● Go around the class asking children to say their full names, and perhaps one or two other things about themselves, for example, their birthday, where they live, how many in their family, whether they have any pets and what their hobbies are. Use this as a basis for discussing the fact that we are all people but are all unique individuals. [1a-d, 2a-b, 3a-b]
● Have a discussion on favourite foods, games, places, or people's likes and dislikes. Ask each child to talk about him/herself, and let the others ask appropriate questions and discuss what has been said. Help children to appreciate that as well as having physical differences, individuals have their own attitudes and feelings. [1a-d, 2a-b, 3a-b]
● Let the children describe their friends, commenting on appearance, personality and whatever else they know about them. Other members of the class could comment on whether the descriptions are accurate. [1a-d, 2a-b, 3a-b]
● Ask the children to talk about the appearance and interests of another unknown member of the class. Let the other children guess the identity of the person being described. [1a-d, 2a-b, 3a-b]
● Communicate using hands and facial expressions only – let the children explore the use of these body parts for expression – and have others talk about and guess the feelings or messages being communicated. [1d]

**Reading**
● Read aloud from stories, poems and rhymes about people and various body parts (faces, eyes, hands, feet, hair, teeth, etc.) [1a, 1c, 1d, 2a, 2b, 2c, 3]
● Help the children to appreciate that being able to read is part of being 'ourselves'. Let them talk about favourite stories, poems and books, explaining why particular pieces of writing are very special to them. [1a, 1c, 1d, 2a, 2b, 2c, 3]

**Writing**
● Write descriptions of other individuals (physical appearance, personality, interests, etc.) for others to read and try to identify. Descriptions may be about classmates, TV or sports personalities, or other well-known people. [1a-c, 2a-e, 3a-b]
● With children in the early stages of writing, draw pictures of people as mentioned above, and write simple words or symbols to express feelings about them. [1a, 1b, 2a, 2b, 2d, 2e, 3a-b]
● Let the children write poems and stories about 'myself', 'my family', or other specific titles such as 'my likes and dislikes', 'my favourite games', 'what I love to eat', 'the best day I have ever had', and so on. [1a-c, 2a-e, 3a-b]
● Write labels for use on displays of various body parts. [1a-c, 2a-e, 3b]
● Write accounts (factual or imaginative) of what it would be like to live without certain body parts – hands, arms, legs – and of the courage and skills developed by handicapped people who are still able to write, paint, take part in sports and so on. [1a-c, 2a-e, 3a-b]

# SCIENCE ▶

**Experimental and investigative science**
All activities in this section provide opportunities for experimental and investigative science.

These activities also overlap and link closely with mathematical activities.

**Life processes and living things**
● Make large collage wall pictures of the human body, labelling head, hair, face, eyes, nose, teeth, hands, arms, legs, feet. Children could be divided into groups, each group to produce a collage of a particular body part and researching/explaining its importance. [1a-b, 2a, 4a-b]

- Write captions and explanations for the above display, reinforcing the importance of separate body parts whilst also developing an appreciation of the interconnectedness that exists among parts of the human body. [1a-b, 2a, 4a-b]
- Extend understanding of the importance and use of various body parts by asking the children to predict and test their ability to perform tasks not usually associated with certain features, for example, ask them to carry things or paint with their feet; to move on body parts other than the feet. [1a-b, 2a, 4a-b]
- Devise a fair test to find out who can see the furthest. Test vision of right eyes, left eyes and both eyes. [1a-b, 2a, 2f, 4a-b]
- Devise similar tests for other bodily functions, for example who has the best sense of hearing, best developed sense of taste, who can run/hop/walk the fastest, etc. [1a-b, 2a, 2f, 4a-b]
- Devise tests to see whether eyes are essential (and similar tests for other body parts). Blindfold the children and investigate how this affects body functioning in various ways, for example, can they still walk in a straight line? Can they eat successfully? [1a-b, 2a, 2f, 4a-b]
- Erect screens in the classroom and devise tests to ascertain whether you can tell the difference between boys and girls by looking only at body parts such as feet, legs, hands, hair and eyes. [1a-b, 2a, 2f, 4a-b]

- Following on from the above, let the children set up investigations to see whether they can identify a particular friend by observing one body feature only. Discuss which features are most helpful for individual identification [1a-b, 2a, 2f, 4a-b]
- Research and where possible test and investigate the role and function of other 'hidden' body parts such as the brain and memory, the digestive system, the heart. Add these to your collage wall display of the human body and add to your annotations by commenting on things necessary to sustain them in a healthy condition. [1a-b, 2a, 2b, 2c, 2d, 2f, 4a-b]
- Make a study of life processes essential to the health of 'ourselves'. [1a-b, 2b, 2c, 2d, 2e, 2f]
- Find out which body parts it is possible to stay alive without – for example, teeth, hair, feet, arms – and those which are absolutely vital for survival. [2a, 2b, 2f]
- Examine the human skeleton by using pictures and models as available from educational suppliers. Study the patterns of bones. Discuss the fact that our bodies have both external features and a crucial internal structure. [1a-b, 2a]
- Find out about and use tests for colour blindness. [1b, 2a, 2f]
- Investigate how we gain some of the features which make up 'ourselves'; for example, inheritance of eye colour. [1b, 2a, 2e, 2f, 4a-b]

## HEALTH EDUCATION ▶

- Talk about how we can see inside the body if necessary, for example, by X-ray or by inserting special instruments. Investigate the role of nurses and doctors in keeping humans healthy.
- Talk and write about how we can look after our 'whole' selves – both internal and external parts. Do this for each body part separately and also consider taking care of the whole body by, for example, keeping warm, having enough rest, exercising regularly, eating a balanced diet, keeping ourselves clean and not doing or swallowing anything that may harm or damage our bodies.

## MATHEMATICS ▶

**Using and applying mathematics**
All activities below provide opportunities for using and applying mathematics.

**Number**
- Do tooth counts. Let the children work in pairs to count the number of teeth in a friend's mouth. Do a survey of the teeth of all members of the class or school. See if they all have the same number. If not, investigate why not. [1a-f, 2a-c, 3c, 4c, 4d, 5b]
- Collect data on such things as body weights, heights, size and area of hands, feet, heads, whole bodies, number of teeth, etc. Draw graphs and other diagrams to represent and interpret these statistics, and design and use appropriate databases. [5b]
- Do an eye colour survey – collect data on children's eye colour from the school as a whole. Find ways of representing this so that comparisons can be made, the most common colour identified, etc. [5b]

- Conduct other surveys on hobbies, pets, birthday months, size of families, how many families living in a certain street have children attending the school, and so on. Represent the results in graphical or diagrammatical form. [5b]
- Take heart and pulse rates. Draw graphs of these in rank order [5b]

**Shape, space and measures**
- Measure various body parts such as hands and feet. Decide how best to do this and ensure uniformity of measurement. Consider sizes of hands, feet, arms, legs, etc. in relation to the body as a whole: for example, measure the height of each child and see whether the tallest children have the largest hands and feet, etc. [4a-b]
- Compare the area of selected body parts. Let each child lie down on squared paper whilst their partner

draws around them. Count squares covered by the whole body; also those covered by separate parts such as head, hands, feet, legs. See if there is a correlation between overall body size and head, hands, feet and leg sizes. [4a-b]

● Devise investigations to see whether children with the largest feet or the longest legs can run the fastest, whether those with the biggest hands or the longest arms can throw the farthest, etc. [4a-b]

● Let the children measure the length of their partner's hair (decide as a class how to do this so that all measurements are fair.) Repeat after a few weeks and compare growth. [4a-b]

# HISTORY

**Areas of study (Key Elements 1-5)**

● Study photographs or pictures of people in the past (at various times, including the recent past as well as long ago). Look at how people have changed their appearance, perhaps according to the fashions of the times. Focus on particular themes – for example, study hairstyles through the ages, clothing, or how people have amused themselves in days gone by. [1a-b]

● Ask the children to bring in old photographs of themselves and family members in the past. Discuss how these can inform us about changes in ourselves and others. [1a-b]

# GEOGRAPHY

**Geographical skills and places**

● Collect pictures/photographs of people from around the world. Make a study of similarities and differences between 'ourselves' and people from other lands, perhaps focusing on specific features such as faces around the world, hairstyles around the world. [1c, 2, 3e, 3f]

# ART

**Investigating and making**

● Draw or paint profiles and/or full-face pictures of other class members. Pay attention to discussion of shape of faces and features, also to shades of colour and details of hairstyle.

● Make pictures with fingerprints and/or footprints.

● Make pictures on the body, i.e. paint faces and hands – using appropriate materials – and with due caution and explanation. Link to studies of hand painting and body painting as a practice in certain cultures and religions.

● Following on from the above, find out how actors and actresses are able to change their appearance to suit the character they are playing. Collect pictures of actors made up for different roles, and perhaps invite a make-up artist to visit the school and talk to the children about his/her work, preferably with a demonstration.

● Design and paint posters about taking care of particular body parts or the body as a whole. Organise a school display on 'Taking Care Of Ourselves'.

● Let each child make a painting or collage of him/herself. Display these together with actual photographs of the children as a class display.

# RE

● Investigate how members of certain racial and religious groups have adopted a particular identity associated with that group, such as a hairstyle.

# P.E.

● Undertake a range of P.E. activities and help children to recognise the effects of physical activity on their bodies. For example, help them to become aware of the changes that happen to their body during exercise (link to Health Education, Science and measurement of heart and pulse rates.)

**Blueprints links**
**Art Key Stage 1:** topic on my family and myself; **Christmas Key Stage 1**, topic on caring; **Early Years Songs and Rhymes:** many songs and rhymes for this topic; **Health Education Key Stage 1:** topics on medicines and drugs, growing up, families, exercising, healthy eating, keeping clean, feeling good; **History Key Stage 1:** topics on family, being a child and many copymasters; **Infant Geography Resource Bank:** copymasters 1–10, 68–74, 91, 93–96; **Infant Teacher's Resource Bank:** the senses (copymaster 131), the body and the skeleton (copymasters 141–142); **The Poetry Book:** topics on family and the senses; **Religious Education Key Stage 1:** topic on big me and little me; **Science Key Stage 1:** many activities and copymasters in life processes and living things section; **Topics Key Stage 1:** topics on my body, and family; **Topics 5–8:** topic on myself; **Writing 5–8:** Copymasters 1–10, 12–14, 21, 40; **Writing Book:** Copymasters 7, 41, 71–5.

# HOMES

## ENGLISH

- Discuss individual homes
- Talk about the meaning of 'home'
- Study different kinds of homes
- Investigate favourite homes
- Read and tell stories/poems about homes
- Study some animal homes
- Write imaginary stories/poems involving a home or homes
- Label display signs
- Record scientific investigations
- Write factual accounts of journeys outside school
- Write about changes in homes and other relevant facts

## HEALTH EDUCATION

- Talk about safety in the home
- Discuss and learn what to do in an emergency

## GEOGRAPHY

- Study large-scale map of local area
- Walk round a planned route
- Look at homes and roads
- Study the local environment
- Talk about people in the locality

## ART

- Make a variety of pictures depicting all kinds of homes, real or imaginary
- Design and make a wall frieze
- Build a road of houses
- Create a picture gallery of homes
- Take rubbings from building materials
- Make a fantasy home
- Look at pictures of homes through the ages

## R.E.

- Talk about the concept of 'home'
- Investigate the meaning of 'refugee'
- Tell or read stories of philanthropists of the past
- Discuss the work of Mother Theresa of Calcutta
- Consider a fund-raising effort for charity
- Investigate the work of Dr Barnardo

## MATHEMATICS

- Study house numbers (odd/even)
- Investigate the need for standard measurements in the home
- Estimate and measure classroom areas
- Study shapes used in building
- Represent data pictorially and on a database

## HISTORY

- Study pictures of homes through the ages
- Write/draw some household items not found in homes, say 100 years ago
- Compare real and fictional homes
- Study homes of the past
- Visit a stately home, or similar
- Discuss how information about the past is obtained

## DESIGN AND TECHNOLOGY

- Design, plan, make and evaluate a model of an ideal home
- Play guessing game – 'Whose House?'
- Prepare a simple database on homes

## SCIENCE

- Investigate a variety of building materials and display these
- Learn about natural and human-made materials
- Test a selection of building materials
- Study weathering on local buildings
- Discuss main causes of weathering
- Talk about heating/lighting in homes
- Learn about fuels, their uses and potential dangers
- Complete an electrical circuit

## IDEAS BANK

General starting points: Suggestions for programmes of study of core and foundation subjects relating to topic, and links with cross-curricular themes and R.E.

## STARTING POINTS

● Let the children draw, write and talk about where they live.
● Show pictures and/or photographs of other people's homes, including famous people such as the Queen, a pop star or a sports personality as well as those lived in by people around us. Discuss similarities and differences.
● Arrange a visit to a stately home of the present or the past (a castle, manor house or similar building). In some areas there may be a special museum of old buildings you could visit, such as Avoncroft, near Bromsgrove in the West Midlands.
● Take the class out for a walk around the local area to look at the different types of homes within it.

# ENGLISH ▶

## Speaking and listening

● Talk about the children's own homes and discuss pictures of other homes which you may have collected – for example, a palace, a narrow boat, a mansion, a cottage, a caravan, and so on. Ask the children where they would like to live and encourage them to give reasons why. Talk about detached, semi-detached, terraced houses and bungalows or flats. [1a-d, 2a-b, 3a-b]
● Let the children work in small groups to plan a story about a home. It may be necessary to give some ideas here, for example, 'The Home That Ran Away' (caravan) or blew away (tent), etc. Let the children tell their stories to the class. [1a-d, 2a-b, 3a-b]
● Read and/or tell stories and poems about homes, including animal homes. Discuss each of these with the class. [1a-d, 2a-b, 3a-b]

## Reading

● Discuss the content and structure of selected stories and poems to encourage and enable children to become involved in reading entire pieces or selected extracts aloud to the class. [1a, 1c, 1d, 2a, 2c, 3]
● Relate a real or imaginary beginning to a story about a home, and ask the children to predict what might happen next and how the story might end. [1a, 1c, 2a, 2b, 2c, 3]

## Writing

● Write imaginary stories about homes, for example, 'The Enchanted Castle'/Tower/Room; 'The Night The Roof Blew Away'; 'Lost on a Houseboat'; 'The King's Dungeon', and so on. [1a-c, 2a-e, 3a-b]
● Make labels and informative signs for displays of, say, building materials or pictures of homes. [1a-c, 2a-e, 3a-b]
● Record in a variety of ways the results of science experiments (see Science activities). [1a-c, 2a-e, 3a-b]
● Ask the children to write factual accounts of any school visit and walk around the local area. Write about the changes in homes over a period of time. [1a-c, 2a-e, 3a-b]

# SCIENCE ▶

## Experimental and investigative science

All activities below provide opportunities for experimental and investigative science.

## Materials and their properties

● Let the children discuss their own homes in specific terms, including materials used in building. Make a display of building materials (brick, slate, tile, concrete, etc.) and ask children to add to this if they can. Explain the need for safety when searching for such materials (children should keep well away from building sites) and suggest that they ask for adult help with collecting/carrying items into school. A local builder may well be able to help by loaning samples of these materials, and may even be prepared to visit the school for a structured talk or interview. [1a-e]
● Talk about and examine the most common materials used in buildings, including the school and local shops. Group any building materials brought for the classroom display into natural or human-made categories. [1a-c]
● Test selected building materials – for example, are they waterproof, will they melt, etc. [1a-e, 2a-b]
● Look at local buildings and observe which materials show signs of weathering – are they natural or human-made? [2a-b]

## Physical processes

● Discuss heating and lighting in homes. If possible, arrange a visit by a representative from the local Gas Board or Electricity Board to talk about their respective services. [1a-c]
● Talk about possible dangers in the home if gas and/or electricity is misused. Using the appropriate equipment (bulb, battery, etc.) let the children experiment and learn how to complete an electrical circuit. [1a-c]

7

# MATTHEMATICS

## Using and applying mathematics
All activities provide opportunities for using and applying mathematics.

## Number
- Talk about house numbers, and investigate odd/even numbers. How many children in the class, or the school, live in evenly numbered houses? How many live in houses with odd numbers? [1a-f, 2a-c, 5b]
- Construct graphs or other diagrams to record information relating to the topic: for example, do children live in detached/semi-detached homes? How many have gardens? How many live in the same street? [1e, 1f, 5a-b]
- Prepare a simple database for each child to show such information as type of house, how many bedrooms, how many windows, colour of front door, odd or even numbered, with or without garage, and so

on. Let the children access this information as required. [1e, 1f, 5a-b]

(NOTE: Deal sensitively with this activity if children are from a wide range of background: some may not have 'regular' homes.)

## Shape, space and measure
- Discuss measurements in children's homes and the need for standard measurements. Let the children estimate the width and length of the classroom, of other areas in the school (including windows, doors, etc.) and of their own homes. They should then check the accuracy of their predictions by measuring. [4a-b]
- Discuss shapes used in buildings (the school, local housing, etc.) Use correct mathematical terms to describe common two-dimensional shapes and three-dimensional objects. [2a-c]

# DESIGN AND TECHNOLOGY

## Design and technology capability
- Discuss different types of houses. Let the children talk about their own homes and then offer suggestions for an 'ideal' house in which they would like to live. [1a-c, 2a-c]

## Designing skills
- Ask the children to discuss, plan, design and draw their own ideal home. [1a-f]

## Making skills and knowledge and understanding
Select and use appropriate materials to construct their planned homes. [4a, 4b, 4c, 4d, 4e, 5a-g]
- Let the children show their models to the class. Discuss each contribution, evaluating the end product. [4f]

## Information technology
- Let the children make 'secret' recordings about 'my home' and ask the other children to guess whose home it is. [1a, 2a]
- Prepare a simple database to show details of individual homes. Include information such as the type of house, number of bedrooms, garage, garden, etc. Help the children to enter data into the computer, and to amend and retrieve information when necessary. By drawing up a suitable questionnaire, this activity could be extended to encompass a survey of the whole school. [1b, 1c, 2a-c, 3a-c]

# ART

## Investigating and making
- Let the children create pictures of imaginary homes and their own houses, using a variety of materials and techniques. Individual rooms could be depicted in diorama form.
- Design a classroom wall frieze of a street showing houses (numbered), shops, etc., or a house in the country, a crooked house, a home on water, a home on stilts, and so on.
- Let the children build a road of houses using cardboard boxes with frontages painted on.
- Create a picture gallery of homes and encourage children to bring in pictures of real or imaginary ones. Discuss these, and let children categorise them if this is feasible.
- Look at the shapes used in building, at patterns and at materials used.

- Take rubbings from appropriate building materials showing different textures. Create a collage building using rubbings.
- A fantasy element might be introduced into art work by asking the children to picture the sort of home a witch, a giant or a vampire, for example, might live in. This could be extended to include famous characters from fiction and/or fairytale, such as Captain Hook, Aladdin, Robin Hood, the Genie of the Lamp, Punch and Judy, the Man in the Moon, Robinson Crusoe and so on.

## Knowledge and understanding
- Discuss the pictures of homes brought into the classroom, and the various techniques such as photography which have been used to depict them.

# GEOGRAPHY

**Geographical skills and places**
- Prepare a large-scale map of the local area. Take the children for a walk around a planned route, and let them follow this route using smaller, individual maps. Encourage them to look and absorb as much information as possible about the homes en route. Discuss such things as 'the largest home', 'the oldest home', 'the best kept home', and so on. [1a, 1b, 2, 3a-f, 4, 5a-d]
- Use the walk and follow-up activities to increase the children's knowledge of their local environment, and in particular its homes. Discuss roads where children live, familiar buildings necessary for the people who live in homes, places where people in the homes shop and work, etc. [1a, 1b, 2, 3a-f, 4, 5a-d]

- Draw attention to the local terrain upon which homes are built (colour of soil, hills, water, etc.). See which homes are on a hillside, on flat land, and so on. [1a, 1b, 2, 3a-f, 4, 5a-d]

**Geographical skills and thematic study**
- Talk about people in the local environment and why they might choose to live where they do. Are the houses round the school part of a small or large settlement? Are the shops a long way from the houses? Discuss local facilities for leisure, travel, etc. [1a-c, 2, 3a-f, 6a-c]
- Encourage children to give their views about the local environment. Can it be improved and, if so, how? What do they like/dislike about living there? [1a, 1b, 2, 6c]

# HISTORY

**Areas of study (Key Elements 1-5)**
- Look at pictures of modern homes, and contrast them with pictures of homes of, say, fifty years ago, a hundred years ago, and so on. On the walk around the local area, look at different styles of houses. Are some older than others? If the answer is yes, how can the children tell? Why do they think this is so? Talk about the differences between homes of many years ago (for example, back-to-back houses) and those of today. A 'Polaroid' camera would be useful to record examples of the different styles of houses encountered on the walk. Sort any pictures of homes and place them in approximate date order. [1a-b]
- Ask the children to collect or draw pictures of modern day household items that would NOT have been found in homes of fifty, or a hundred or more years ago. What would life have been like without them? [1a-b]

- Look at some of the pictures and/or photographs of real homes and compare these with pictures of fictitious homes in story books – for example, 'Three Little Pigs', 'Little House On The Prairie', 'Wind In The Willows', etc. [1a-b]
- From a range of visual resources – for example, artists' pictures, photographs of cave homes (including those of long ago and the recently restored Kinver Edge cave house), castles, Tudor houses, huts, and so on – discuss homes in the past. Help the children to extract as much information as possible about these homes and the people who lived there. [1a-b]
- Talk about making historical deductions and assumptions from limited sources, for example, about the early inhabitants of Britain and how they lived. This can lead into a discussion on artefacts and relics from the past, and differences between past and present times. [1a-b]

# R.E.

- Discuss the concept of a house as a safe haven or refuge, and talk about people who have no home, perhaps as a result of war, poverty or other misfortune. Introduce the word 'refugee' and discuss its meaning.
- Tell the class about the wretched lives of many working class children in Victorian times, and of living conditions in those days. Read about and research the efforts of philanthropists of the time such as Dr John Barnardo, who dedicated much of his life to giving shelter to homeless boys in London. Remind the children

that Dr Barnardo's work still continues today, through the efforts of the charity that bears his name.
- Tell the children about Sister Theresa of Calcutta, who has spent her life helping the poor, the sick and the homeless, and of the many others who work tirelessly to help those in need.
- A practical outcome to this topic could be a fund-raising effort resulting in a donation to an appropriate charity or an international relief organisation.

# HEALTH EDUCATION

- Discuss all aspects of safety in the home, including the care needed when dealing with electricity and gas.

Talk about what to do in an emergency, and perhaps how to telephone for help.

**Blueprints links**
**Art Key Stage 1:** complete topic on homes, copymasters 25–37; **Art Resource Bank** copymasters 92–99; **Christmas Key Stage 1:** play on homes; **Distant Places:** Corfu copymasters 5, 6, San Francisco copymaster 6; **Early Years Songs and Rhymes:** many songs and rhymes on the topic; **History Key Stage 1:** topic on homes in history and many copymasters; **Geography Key Stage 1:** copymasters 7 (street survey), 32–3, 67, 72–5, 77–80 (house model); **Infant Geography Resource Bank:** section on homes and settlements, copymasters 1–10;

**Infant Teacher's Resource Bank:** copymasters 115, 116 (types of home), 133 (animal homes); **Health Education Key Stage 1:** copymasters 31, 33; **Religious Education Key Stage 1:** copymaster 42; **Science Key Stage 1:** activities and copymasters in Materials and their properties; **Second Key Stage 1 Topic Book:** topic on buildings with copymasters; **Technology Key Stage 1:** many activities and copymasters; **Topics 5–8:** complete topic on homes with copymasters; **Writing 5–8:** copymasters 3, 5, 8, 24, 31–4, 37, 46, 49, 51, 55; **Writing Book:** copymaster 39.

# COLOUR

**COLOUR**

## ENGLISH

- Discuss favourite colours
- Read or tell stories and poems which involve colour
- Write imaginative stories and poems linked with colour
- Make lists of one-colour items
- Learn the colours of the rainbow
- Label classroom displays
- Undertake personal reflective writing
- Record details of scientific investigations
- Write factually about colour

## MATHEMATICS

- Use mathematical shapes to make colour patterns
- Learn about halves and quarters
- Devise repeat patterns
- Learn correct mathematical names for two-dimensional shapes and three-dimensional objects
- Investigate reflective symmetry
- Find out about tessellations
- Discuss angles in relation to shapes
- Represent data pictorially and on a database

## R.E.

- Read or tell the stories of Joseph and Noah's Ark
- Discuss the concept of jealousy

## HISTORY

- Learn about photography
- Discuss pictures and photographs
- Investigate pictures from the past
- Learn about William the Conqueror and the Bayeux Tapestry
- Make a sequence picture-story

## GEOGRAPHY

- Investigate colour in the local area
- Research colour in relation to seasons

## P.E.

- Create a 'mood' dance linked with colour

## HEALTH EDUCATION

- Investigate colours of everyday signs
- Talk about the dangers of the sun's rays

## DESIGN AND TECHNOLOGY

- Organise single-colour displays
- Design, plan, make and evaluate a model 'ideal colour' classroom
- Publish a holiday news sheet
- Construct simple database for storage and retrieval of colour data

## MUSIC

- Use instruments to make 'colour' sounds
- Compose pieces of music depicting a colour
- Learn songs about colour
- Listen to selected pieces of music by well-known composers

## ART

- Make a wide variety of colour pictures
- Design a rainbow wall frieze
- Learn about primary colours and paint-mixing
- Make dyes from natural materials
- Use tie and dye techniques
- Look at a wide range of pictures

## SCIENCE

- Observe colour within the classroom
- Look at colour in nature
- Learn about natural materials
- Consider the importance of sun and light in relation to colour

**IDEAS BANK**

General starting points: Suggestions for programmes of study of core and foundation subjects relating to topic, and links with cross-curricular themes and R.E.

**STARTING POINTS**

● Have pre-arranged groups of articles in one-colour sets on display in the classroom. Let the children talk about why they are so arranged.

● Show rainbow pictures and identify the seven colours.

● Show the children black and white and coloured pictures and/or photographs. Discuss colour – is it important? Can you learn more about a picture if it is in colour?

● Let the children list as many items as they can which are all the same colour. Continue by listing another colour, then another and so on, in order to focus thoughts onto colour. Display each list.

# ENGLISH ▶

**Speaking and listening**

● Talk about everyone's favourite colour, and discuss the least popular colour(s). Can children suggest reasons why some colours are more popular than others? Do colours affect how we feel? [1a-d, 2a-b, 3a-b]

● Let the children work in groups or individually to think of as many green/yellow/red/etc things as possible. Make lists of these, and ask the children to write and/or draw the things on their lists. [1a, 1b, 1c, 2a-b, 3a-b]

● Read or tell poems and/or stories involving colour. Talk about these with the class. Discuss well-known phrases or sayings about colour – for example, 'red with rage', 'blue with cold', 'green with envy', 'white as a sheet', etc. [1a-d, 2a-b, 3a-b]

● Arrange for the children to work in groups or pairs to plan an imaginary story involving colour – for example, 'The Yellow Dog', 'How The Flowers Lost Their Colour', and so on. When the stories are ready, let the children tell them to each other. [1a-d, 2a-b, 3a-b]

**Reading**

● Work with the class to create an imaginary beginning to a story about colour, for example, a rainbow that loses/changes its colour. Ask the children to write/draw their own middle and ending to the story. Let them read their stories aloud to the class when they are complete. If children can only write a few words, let them read these and tell the rest of their story through a sequence of pictures. [1a, 1c, 1d, 2a, 2b, 2c, 3]

**Writing**

● Draw/write imaginary stories/poems involving colour, for example, 'The Dragon Who Turned Blue' 'When Mum's/Dad's Hair Turned Green', and so on. [1a-c, 2a-e, 3a-b]

● Make labels for colour displays, some giving brief relevant information. [1a-c, 2a-e, 3a-b]

● Record details of Science experiments on colour. [1a-c, 2a-e, 3a-b]

● Write a factual account of a walk round the local area (see Geography activities). [1a-c, 2a-e, 3a-b]

# SCIENCE ▶

**Experimental and investigative science**

All activities below provide opportunities for experimental and investigative science.

● Let the children look at, and feel, different kinds of single-coloured materials. Discuss them – for example, are they soft/hard, warm/cold, natural/man-made, etc.? And does colour affect how they feel? Does colour affect the children's predictions – for example, do they think red material will feel warm? [1a, 1b, 1c, 4a-b]

● Look at individual colours through different coloured transparencies and/or coloured gelatines. Will the colours appear to change? Encourage children to predict whether or not there will be a colour change, and talk about their findings. [1a, 1b, 1c, 2a, 4a-b]

● Let the children mix various coloured paints, and see if any of the resulting shades match the colours

created by the transparencies. Talk about the primary colours. [1a, 1b, 1c, 2a, 4a-b]

**Materials and their properties**

● Discuss colour in nature. Let the children experiment (with careful supervision) in making dyes from natural materials such as onion skins, elderberries and so on. [1a-c, 2a-b]

● Let children use charcoal, chalk and other natural materials for drawing and painting. Discuss these natural materials. [1a-e, 2a-b]

**Physical processes**

● Talk about the sun and light, and their role in making colour in our world. Let the children look at shadows. Investigate the passage of light. Use prisms, glass, sunlight and water to view the spectrum. [3a-b)]

# MATHEMATICS

## Using and applying mathematics
All activities below provide opportunities for using and applying mathematics

## Number
- Use two-dimensional shapes to investigate halves and quarters while designing colour patterns. [2c]
- Using selected colours, devise repeat patterns with two-dimensional shapes. [3a]
- Let the children sort shapes and describe the criteria chosen. [5a]
- Ask children to construct graphs/diagrams to show the most popular colour in class, the eye or hair colour of the children, and so on. Begin with a class discussion about ways of recording facts and/or information. Let the children work in small groups to design their own graph/diagram, and then collect and enter their chosen information when ready. [1e,5b]
- Structure a simple database so that each child can include such information as colour of eyes/hair, favourite colour, etc. Give the children instruction and practice in entering/retrieving information from the database. [1e,1f,5b]

## Shape, space and measures
- Let children choose which shapes and colour(s) of paper they will use and how they are going to make patterns and repeat patterns with two-dimensional shapes. [2a-c]
- Encourage children to discuss the use of colour in the above activities with the teacher and the rest of the class. [2a-c]
- Use mathematical terms to describe common two-dimensional coloured shapes and three-dimensional objects. [2a-c]
- Investigate reflective symmetry – for example, are both halves of a shape always identical? [2c]
- Which shapes tessellate? Make patterns with coloured sticky paper, for example, design a floor covering. Use one or two colours only. Talk to the children about angles and angling shapes to right/left. [2a-c, 3a-b]

# DESIGN AND TECHNOLOGY

## Design and technology capability
- Ask the children to look at the colours used in their school building, including their classroom surroundings. Do they like the colours? Discuss possible alternatives. Arrange a one-colour display area, change this to another colour after a short period of time, then another. [1a-c]

## Designing skills
- In groups or individually, ask the children to draw/design/talk about a model classroom, using colours of their choice. [2a-c, 3a-f]

## Making skills and knowledge and understanding
- Giving children as wide a choice of materials as possible, let them construct a model classroom, using a large cardboard box as the room itself. Let the children make some model tables, cupboards and so on before deciding what colours they are going to use for walls, ceiling, and furniture, and finally painting the model. [4a, 4b, 4c, 4d, 4e, 5a-g]
- When work is finished, let the children talk about and evaluate all models. Include discussions on materials used and chosen colours. [4f]
- Construct a simple database showing, amongst other things, each child's preference for colours used for, say, walls, ceiling, and so on. [2a-c]

# ART

## Investigating and making
- Let the children paint pictures of their own choice or on a particular theme. When the pictures are completed, talk about the colours used.
- Experiment by asking children to use one chosen colour only for a painting. Discuss the results.
- Design a wall frieze relating to colour, for example, Noah's Ark and the rainbow.
- Explore mixing colours and talk about the wide range of colours which can be obtained by mixing.

Introduce the word 'shades' and use paint charts or similar to illustrate how many shades of one colour are possible.
- Encourage children to be aware of colour in any form of art work undertaken. Look at colour in nature as well as in people-made materials.
- Experiment, under careful supervision, with making dyes from natural materials. Use tie and dye techniques for pictures or collage.
- Make pictures using pattern and colour.

### Knowledge and Understanding

- Collect as many pictures as possible, including some by well-known artists and discuss the use of colour in each of them. Arrange a picture gallery.
- Try to obtain prints of pictures by Piet Mondrian. Discuss these and let children create their own pictures using cubes/rectangles.
- If possible, obtain pictures of cave paintings. Talk about these and look at colours used by early man. Where would the artist's materials come from?

- When talking about the pictures, discuss similarities and differences. Introduce the concept of 'mood' – does a picture make the children feel happy or sad? Talk about this. Do their feelings relate to the colours used?
- Discuss children's own work in relation to other paintings. Include their 'best' pictures in the gallery. Are these chosen because of the effects of colours or other criteria?

# GEOGRAPHY ▶

### Geographical skills and places

- Take the children for a walk round the local area, let them follow a simple map of the route. Ask them to look for colour on their walk, both natural and man-made. If possible, collect natural materials to make dyes. [3b-e,4]
- Whilst on the walk with the children, point out any other well-known features of the local area and talk about these later. Let the children mark them on their maps. Do any features stand out because of their colour? [3a-e,4,5a]
- Talk about colour in relation to the seasons – for example, does each season seem to have particular colours associated with it? [4,5c]

# HISTORY ▶

### Areas of study (Key Elements 1-5)

- Show children a selection of colour photographs depicting life today; compare these with early sepia/black and white photographs. Discuss the differences between actual paintings/prints and photographs. [1a-b]
- Discuss traditional usage of colour in terms of uniforms and equipment – for example, policemen, nurses, pillar boxes, army camouflage jackets, zebra crossings, etc. [1a-b]
- If possible, show children copies of early cave pictures with reference to the colours used. Talk about where early people might have obtained the colours used. [1a-b]

- Show the children some pictures of the Bayeux Tapestry, and look at the colours used. Tell the story of William the Conqueror, look at some of the important details shown in the Tapestry and discuss how the Norman version of the story might be different from that of the Saxons. [2,3]
- Discuss the Bayeux Tapestry and one or two other real-life happenings that are shown in pictures. What do these pictorial representations tell us about life in other times? [1b,2,3]
- Let the children do their own coloured picture story of an important event in their lives. Ask them to include detail such as the clothes they were wearing, the background to the story, and so on. [1a,]

# MUSIC ▶

### Performing and composing

- Talk about colours – do they suggest mood, emotions, dynamics (for example, red is loud, green is quiet, etc.)
- Let the children improvise colour sounds, suggest changing from one colour to another in a continuous pattern. Show children how to record these as colour signs and let them play each other's patterns.
- Learn songs related to the theme of this topic – for example, 'I Can Sing A Rainbow', or songs with a colour in the title such as 'When The Red, Red Robin Comes Bob, Bob, Bobbing Along', 'Lily The Pink', 'Green Grow The Rushes-O', 'Yellow Submarine', 'Yellow Bird', etc.

- Suggest that the children work in pairs/small groups to compose a colour(s) or rainbow piece of music. Let the children record their compositions and play them for others to hear.

### Listening and appraising

- Let the children listen to selected passages of music and talk about them. Do they suggest a mood or colour? What is the rhythm of the music? Which instruments can children hear?
- Use appropriate music for movement and dance, for example, Ravel's 'Bolero'. Does this piece of music suggest a colour? Can the children begin to dance as a

pale shade of colour and then let this colour get darker as the dance progresses? Introduce concepts of structure, pace, and dynamics by letting the children listen to the music and discuss it using their own words.

- Discuss sounds, rhythms, etc. in other pieces of contrasting music – perhaps 'Mars' from Holst's 'Planets Suite', Gounod's 'Funeral March Of A Marionette', or Strauss's 'Thunder And Lightning Polka'.

# P.E.

**Dance**
- Use the children's own musical compositions and other selected music to encourage them to explore and

interpret the different rhythms, moods, etc. of the compositions.

# R.E.

- Tell the children the Old Testament stories of Noah's Ark and Joseph with his coat of many colours.

Discuss jealousy (as it affected the behaviour of Joseph's brothers) and its dangers.

# HEALTH EDUCATION

- As a class, talk about which colours are used in signs (for example, the lollipop person's sign, a halt sign, and so on). Talk about 'Red for Danger' – is this the best colour to use? Why? Mention the Red Cross – why red? Reinforce the correct use of traffic light signals and pedestrian crossings, and emphasize the importance of taking heed of all warning signs.

- Discuss the importance of not looking directly into the sun when talking about sun and light. It is also an opportunity to warn children about the dangers of too much sun – for example, sunstroke and sunburn, etc.

**Blueprints links**
**Art Key Stage 1:** complete topic on colour, many copymasters; **Assemblies 5–8:** complete photocopiable assembly on colour; **Environmental Education Key Stage 1:** copymaster 25 (rainbow whirler); **Easter:** Easter time copymasters 5–6; **Festivals:** many colour activities involving festivals; **Infant Teacher's Resource**

**Bank:** copymasters 79–84, 144, (colours of the rainbow); **Poetry Book:** copymaster 54; **Religious Education Key Stage 1:** copymasters 57, 63, 106; **Science Key Stage 1:** activities in physical processes, copymasters 48, 77–79; **Second Key Stage 1 Topics Book:** topic on light with copymasters; **Topics 5–8:** complete topic on colour and shape with copymasters.

# TRANSPORT

## SCIENCE

- Observe transport forms
- Consider how they work
- Discuss meaning of 'transport'
- Sort forms into sets
- Devise experiments on transport design
- Construct various transport forms
- Compare use of various materials
- Assess designs
- Test variables in movement
- Study forms of energy and power
- Consider forces
- Move heavy objects
- Investigate power sources

## GEOGRAPHY

- Study route maps
- Draw transport maps
- Study aerial photographs
- Spot evidence of transport
- Study transport around the world
- Consider transport elsewhere in UK
- Explain why various forms are used
- Study movement of goods
- Study local services
- Investigate journeys

## ART

- Create a variety of individual pictures relating to transport
- Design and make a 'transport wall frieze'
- Make clay models
- Study relevant pictures by various artists
- Look at modern/historical advertisements relating to transport

## MUSIC

- Use instruments to create transport 'sounds' and to compose relevant music
- Learn a selection of songs linked with transport
- Listen to relevant recorded music, classical, traditional and modern and discuss this

## ENVIRONMENTAL EDUCATION

- Investigate transport-related pollution
- Consider impact on environment

**TRANSPORT**

## HISTORY

- Study earliest transport forms
- Study history and development of transport
- Investigate invention of the wheel
- Make a time line
- Read stories of people associated with transport
- Debate modern transport
- Discuss stories of people, journeys, events
- Visit a museum
- Conduct interviews
- Study photographs and artefacts

## HEALTH EDUCATION

- Reinforce road safety
- Study transport safety
- Make a safety frieze
- Study 'emergency' transport
- Learn to be safe
- Study Green Cross Code and Highway Code
- Talk about playing in safe/dangerous places

## MATHEMATICS

- Predict outcome of investigations
- Test predictions
- Measure and weigh any items being tested
- Look at shapes used for making models
- Sort models into sets
- Compare and order models without measuring
- Investigate probability
- Represent data pictorially and on a database

## ENGLISH

- Study and discuss toys and books brought into school
- Talk about different modes of transport
- Read and tell stories/poems linked with transport
- Write/draw imaginary stories linked with topic
- Record details of scientific investigations
- Label classroom displays and write informative captions
- Write factually about school visit(s), history of transport and any other relevant information
- Use reference books to find out information

## DESIGN AND TECHNOLOGY

- Discuss making working transport models
- Design, plan, make and evaluate a working model
- Structure a simple data base
- Use other methods of recording statistical information

16

**IDEAS BANK**
General starting points: Suggestions for programmes of study of core and foundation subjects relating to topic, and links with cross-curricular themes and R.E.

**STARTING POINTS**
● Ask the children to bring in their model boats, cars, trains and planes. Make a display of these and let the children show how they work, and perhaps play with them in groups.
● Visit a museum such as a railway, maritime or general transport museum.
● Visit a show such as a motor show, or boat show.
● Go for an eye-spy walk into your local area; see how many different forms of transport the children can spot.
● Go for a ride on one or more forms of transport; perhaps a train, bus or boat.

● Visit a railway station, bus station, underground station, ferry terminal, port or airport.
● Ask the children for their definitions of 'transport' and then, in simple terms, tell them the accurate meaning of the word ('to carry across'), include road, sea and air transport.
● Arrange a display of pictures showing various methods of transport used today. Look at books, video tape recordings etc., which show transport now and earlier methods of conveyancing. Discuss these with the children and encourage them to bring in their own books, pictures and so on for discussion and display.
● Tell or read stories involving transport, for example, 'The Railway Cat', 'The Railway Children', 'The Mice and the Clockwork Bus'.

# ENGLISH ▶

**Speaking and listening**
● As a class, discuss the different modes of transport used by the children. Talk about when they are used and why different forms of transport might be used. [1a, 1c]
● Let the children work in small groups to plan an imaginary story involving a specified form of transport. When they are ready, let them tell, or act, their stories to the rest of the class. [1a-d, 2a-b]

**Reading**
● Discuss the content of relevant stories and poems read and/or told to the children. Where appropriate let individual children read a short story or poem to the class. [1a, 1c-d]
● Work with the children to produce the beginning of a story involving transport, ask them to predict what might happen next and how the story will end. Ask them to write and/or draw their own middle and/or end and then read or tell their story to the rest of the class. [1a, 1c-d]
● Encourage children to select information from any books they have brought into school, or alternatively from school reference books, and, where appro-

priate, let them read this aloud to the other children. Follow this with a class discussion. Where children are not yet confident enough, or able, to read the information aloud, let them work with you to hold the book, point to the appropriate page and pass on their chosen information to the rest of the class. This should be a purely voluntary exercise by the child concerned. [1b, 2d]

**Writing**
● Let the children write/draw imaginary stories involving some form of transport, for example, 'A Bike for a Present', 'Adventure in an Aeroplane', 'The Day the Bus Got Lost', and so on. [1a-c, 2a-b]
● Make labels and write information about a class display of toy transport vehicles, planes and so on, brought in by the children. [1a-c]
● Record details of any scientific investigations. [1a-c]
● Write factual accounts of any school visits. [1a-c]
● Write factually about specified aspects of transport, possibly including early pioneers of, say, steam transport, aviation and so on. [1a-c]

# MATHEMATICS ▶

**Using and applying mathematics**
● Encourage children to select the appropriate materials and mathematics as required when making/testing models of transport vehicles. [1a-b, 2a-d]
● Let the children predict the outcomes of tests and discuss all work both as a class and individually. [1a-b, 2a-d, 3c-d, 4a]

**Number**
● Measure length and weight of selected models, e.g. cars, lorries, boats and so on.
Test them for speed of movement. Do children consider length/weight relevant to performance? [1a, 1c, 4a-b]

● Construct graphs, diagrams and/or charts to show which methods of transport have been used by the children, their favourite form of transport, how they come to school, (this could be a whole school survey) and so on. [5a-b]
● Design a simple data collection sheet for specified information, for example details of transport models, how they were built to move, materials used and so on. Access this information using simple data bases and give children practice in selecting and retrieving information. [5a-b]
● Investigate probability; for example, it is certain/uncertain that this car will move along the

ground if pushed, but impossible for it to fly up into space. [5a-b]

**Shape, space and measures**
- Let the children compare and order their models without measuring. [1a, 4a]
- Discuss models made by the children and talk about the shapes used in their making. Name the shapes. [1a, 2a]
- Use mathematical terms to describe common two-dimensional shapes and three dimensional objects used when making models. [1a, 2b]

# DESIGN AND TECHNOLOGY

**Designing skills**
- Discuss the possibility of making individual transport vehicles, which can move in various ways. Investigate the realities of the children's ideas and/or proposals. Do not commence this until the children have discussed various methods which can be used to create movement, for example wheels/axle, air-power, magnetic force, and so on. Let them examine, (under supervision) some of the toys on display to see how movement is achieved. [3a-b]
- Talk about, plan and design individually or in pairs three-dimensional transport models. [3a-f]

**Making skills and knowledge and understanding**
- Help the children to work individually or in pairs to finalise plans/designs and make models using appropriate materials and tools. Be aware of safety issues at all times. [4a-e]
- Let all the children evaluate the results of their model-making with both teacher and their peers in class. [4f]

# INFORMATION TECHNOLOGY

- Construct simple data collection sheet(s) to show selected details about transport, the most used mode by children, the most popular colour car and so on. Give children practice in entering, amending and retrieving this information.[1a, 2a-c]

- Discuss other methods of recording statistical information, such as graphs, pie charts, pictograms, etc.

# ART

**Investigating and making**
- Use a wide variety of materials and techniques to enable the children to produce a varied range of pictures about their transport topic. Encourage them to discuss each completed piece of work.
- Help the children to design a wall frieze, this could either depict one form of transport, say, on land or could incorporate all forms of conveyance. Ensure that all children contribute to the overall result.

- Let the children use clay to model either a land vehicle or a boat/aeroplane.

**Knowledge and understanding**
- Look at a variety of pictures relating to the topic, including, if possible, some historical ones. Discuss how various artists have depicted travel/transport. Look also for art in the local environment in the form of advertisements. Talk about these and compare with more traditional paintings.

# MUSIC

**Performing and composing**
- Discuss different modes of transport and let the children experiment with a variety of instruments to convey aeroplanes, trains, trucks, cars etc.

- Encourage children to compose their own music linked to one or more of these themes. Let them play and record their music, and discuss it with the class.

- Learn some songs which are relevant to the topic, for example, 'Daisy Bell' (bicycle) 'The Runaway Train'; 'Jogging up and Down' and 'What Would Make Me Happy' (wagon, aeroplane, car, tractor) – both these songs from 'Kokoleoko' by June Tillman, published by Macmillan Education. Other songs might include 'Magic Canoe', 'Siren Song' (ship) 'Starship Silver Grey', 'I Built a Rocket', all from 'Phantasmagoria' by Kaye Umansky, publisher A & C Black.

- Discuss why there are so many songs both traditional and modern which have a 'transport' theme. Play some relevant music to the children without revealing titles and let them guess what transport is represented. Discuss sounds, rhythms, etc.
- Let the children listen to selected passages of descriptive music such as 'Coronation Scot'. Talk about each piece of music, the instruments used, the rhythms within the piece and its mood, etc.

# SCIENCE

### Experimental and investigative science
- Observe a range of forms of transport, perhaps by going on an eye-spy walk, taking rides or visiting a transport terminal as suggested in 'Starting Points'. Remind children that the word transport means 'to carry across'. Discuss basic ideas deriving from observations e.g. transport can take us over land, underground, over water, through the air. Consider how transport forms 'work'. [2a]
- Extend the above by sorting transport forms observed (in pictures or real life) into sets; according to where they operate, and suggest how they move, e.g. most land transport forms have wheels, most water transport floats on the surface, most air transport forms have wings. [2a-c]
- Design a series of activities and experiments which demonstrate aspects of the design of various forms of transport, and the sources of power they use. Consult some of the many published science activity books available on such topics as 'flight', 'energy' 'transport', etc. For each activity, ensure that the children suggest ideas and make predictions which can be tested in a fair way. Possible activities include: make a hovercraft or other vessel that will move across water; demonstrate air power by releasing air from a blown up balloon; make and fly kites; design and construct a glider; make steam to turn a paper-wheel. [1a-c, 2a-c]
- Construct transport forms such as boats and kites out of a variety of materials. Design investigations to

see which materials are best suited to the task. [1a-c, 2a-c, 3a]
- Plan and conduct experiments which investigate how the design of particular forms of transport affects their successful operation (e.g. test the effectiveness of boats with and without keels; and sails of various sizes and shapes). [1a-c, 2a-c, 3a]
- Test a variety of variables associated with the movement of toy cars and trains (e.g. move them over differing surfaces, on slopes of various angles, etc. [1a-c, 2a-c, 3a-e]

### Physical processes
- Help children to appreciate that all forms of transport are powered by some form of energy. Make a collection of pictures of vehicles. Sort into sets according to where they operate (land, air, water) and the form of energy they use. In association with this, introduce basic vocabulary such as push, pull, move, force, speed up, slow down. [2a-c]
- Following on from the above and from the construction of gliders and kites, discuss the various forces that enable things to fly through the air. [2a-c]
- Talk about how one might move very heavy objects more easily than by carrying them. Move heavy objects with the help of rollers (carefully supervised). [2a-c]
- Investigate sources of power. Make an illustrated display of transport forms labelled with all the sources of power that are employed to make them move. [2a-c]

# GEOGRAPHY

### Geographical skills
- Use maps of various scales and sizes which show transport routes, e.g. look for the path of a railway line or the location of a station on a map of the local area. [3e]
- Make maps of short routes in your locality, showing the route taken by a form of transport e.g. journey of a bus from school to the shopping centre, journey of a bicycle from home to the park. [3d]
- Look at aerial photographs of your town or locality. Identify features which indicate the presence of transport (e.g. roads, railway line, car parks). (3f)

### Places and themes
- Go out or look at maps to spot evidence of transport in your local area. Ask the children to try to think why transport-related features are located where they are, e.g. why car parks are in certain locations, why the airport is not in the middle of town. [4, 5a, 5d]
- Do a sub-topic on 'transport around the world'. Investigate forms of transport used in other lands, and compare with the UK. Suggest why transport forms differ in various locations. [4, 5a, 5d]
- Compare and contrast transport forms used in different locations in the UK. Consider why, for exam-

ple, London has an underground train system whilst villages and many towns do not. [4, 5a, 5d]
● Investigate and explain why different forms of transport are used. Make an illustrated and annotated frieze explaining as many reasons as you can think of (e.g. to move animals, people and goods, to help in emergencies, to provide services, for recreational purposes). [4, 5a]
● Find out what goods are moved in and out of your home town/village by various forms of transport. [4, 5a-b]

● Make a list or write out local services provided by transport, e.g. police, fire, ambulance, refuse collection, road sweeping, milk delivery. [4, 5b]
● Relate forms of transport to journeys of different lengths. Discuss, for example, which forms are most suitable for very long/very short journeys; journeys across different terrains. Relate to why people make journeys of differing lengths. [4, 5a-b]

# HISTORY ▶

### Range and depth of historical knowledge and understanding
● Make and annotate an illustrated time line of transport (or one of its forms) on the classroom wall, indicating key inventions and landmarks in its development. [1a-b]
● Investigate the world's earliest transport forms, including the use of animals, design of early vessels to cross water, etc. [2a-b]
● Tell the children the story of the invention of the wheel, and help them to understand the great significance of this. [2a]
● Study the history of transport. Find out about key events and inventions. Either do this in general terms, or focus on one aspect such as the history of flight, of railways, of ships, etc. [2a-c]
● Collect as many pictures as possible of transport forms in days gone by. Again, these may be general, or relate to one aspect of the topic. Place them in chronological order and discuss changes that have taken place through time. [1a-b, 2a-c]
● Read stories and factual accounts about the lives of well-known people associated with the history of transport and related inventions. [2a-b]

● Organise a class debate about the pros and cons of modern transport compared to its earlier forms. Consider, for example, what impacts the mass use of the motor car, and extensive development of fast travel by air and rail have had on people and the world. [2a-c]

### Interpretations of history
● Tell stories about well known historic journeys, events and people whose names are associated with the development of transport in one or more of its forms. Talk about the stories. Decide whether two accounts about a particular journey, person or event tell the same version of what happened. [3a]

### Historical enquiry
● Visit a museum of transport, either a general museum or one specific to a form you are studying. Use this as a key resource for classroom development. [4a-b]
● Interview people who can remember forms of transport in days gone by e.g. steam trains, wartime planes. [4a-b]
● Ask elderly friends and relatives if they can lend any photographs or artefacts relating to the history of transport for a carefully supervised classroom display. [4a-b]

# ENVIRONMENTAL EDUCATION ▶

● Do a sub-topic on pollution related to the present day use of transport. Consider forms of pollution (harmful gases, noise] that are associated with transport. Discuss such things as the use of lead-free petrol. Whilst children will not appreciate the science related to this, they may be aware that it is more 'environmentally friendly'.

● Investigate how transport has made an impact on the environment. Perhaps there are examples that could be studied in your local area e.g. construction of a new road, siting of a new airport, a road-widening scheme. Debate whether such impacts are good or bad.

# HEALTH EDUCATION ▶

● Do a special study of safety relating to transport if you are going out on visits. Perhaps focus on a particular aspect, e.g. road safety, safety at the railway station.
● Make a large illustrated frieze relating to transport safety, perhaps writing out rules which are

specific to various transport forms that have been illustrated, e.g. 'always put on your car seat belts' 'cross the road carefully and in a safe place', 'never stand close to the edge of a railway platform', 'always listen to safety instructions on an aircraft'. (Remind children that rear seat belts should be worn in cars as well as front ones.)

● Make a study of how transport can be critical in keeping people healthy and saving lives. Find out more about the work of ambulance rescue services, lifeboat crews, etc.

● Reinforce rules about never getting in to a transport form, e.g. car or lorry, with a stranger.

● Learn The Green Cross Code. Introduce and study The Highway Code.

● Talk about playing in safe/dangerous places/including railway embankments and railway lines in the 'danger zones'.

**Blueprints links**
**Art Key Stage 1:** complete topic on transport and art, many copymasters **Art Resource Bank:** chapter on transport, copymasters 102, 104–105, 107–110; **Distant Places:** Japan copymaster 6; **Early Years Songs and Rhymes:** many songs and rhymes on the topic; **Geography Key Stage 1:** many copymasters throughout, especially journeys copymasters 91–100; **Health Education Key Stage 1:** topic on being safe (road safety), copymasters: 40, 41, 80; **History Key Stage 1:** complete topic on transport in history and many copymasters; **Infant Geography Resource Bank:** section on moving around, copymasters 75–81; **Infant Teacher's Resource Bank:** copymasters 119, 120 (pictures of forms of transport); **Poetry Book:** section on wheels, copymasters 29–32; **Science Key Stage 1:** activities and copymasters in Physical processes 71–75; **Technology Key Stage 1:** many activities and copymasters; **Topics 5–8:** complete topic on transport with copymasters; **Writing 5–8:** copymasters 9, 10, 42–6, 50, 51, 54, 61, 62.

# SEASONS

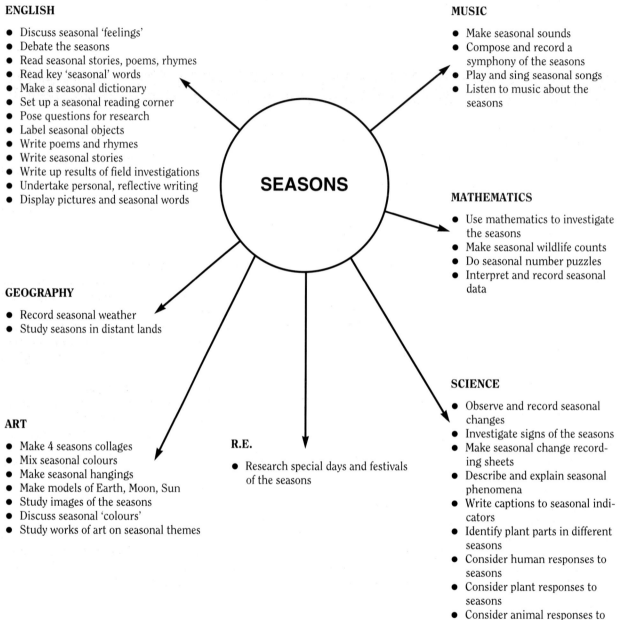

**ENGLISH**

- Discuss seasonal 'feelings'
- Debate the seasons
- Read seasonal stories, poems, rhymes
- Read key 'seasonal' words
- Make a seasonal dictionary
- Set up a seasonal reading corner
- Pose questions for research
- Label seasonal objects
- Write poems and rhymes
- Write seasonal stories
- Write up results of field investigations
- Undertake personal, reflective writing
- Display pictures and seasonal words

**GEOGRAPHY**

- Record seasonal weather
- Study seasons in distant lands

**ART**

- Make 4 seasons collages
- Mix seasonal colours
- Make seasonal hangings
- Make models of Earth, Moon, Sun
- Study images of the seasons
- Discuss seasonal 'colours'
- Study works of art on seasonal themes

**R.E.**

- Research special days and festivals of the seasons

**MUSIC**

- Make seasonal sounds
- Compose and record a symphony of the seasons
- Play and sing seasonal songs
- Listen to music about the seasons

**MATHEMATICS**

- Use mathematics to investigate the seasons
- Make seasonal wildlife counts
- Do seasonal number puzzles
- Interpret and record seasonal data

**SCIENCE**

- Observe and record seasonal changes
- Investigate signs of the seasons
- Make seasonal change recording sheets
- Describe and explain seasonal phenomena
- Write captions to seasonal indicators
- Identify plant parts in different seasons
- Consider human responses to seasons
- Consider plant responses to seasons
- Consider animal responses to seasons
- Find out how and why seasons occur

**IDEAS BANK**
General starting points: Suggestions for programmes of study of core and foundation subjects relating to topic, and links with cross-curricular themes and R.E.

**STARTING POINTS**
● Make a collection of poems, stories and rhymes about seasons of the year.
● Collect pictures from magazines which have a 'seasonal' feel.

● Go out to a park, woodland, farm, hedgerow or into the school grounds to make seasonal observations.
● Discuss and measure changing weather patterns and length of daylight.

(NOTE: Throughout this topic, suggested activities refer to studying 'the seasons' in general. Clearly most of them can be applied to the study of a single season if this is the focus of your topic.)

# SCIENCE

**Experimental and investigative science**
All activities marked with an asterisk below provide opportunities for experimental and investigative science.
● *At key times in the year when the seasons show signs of change, observe the world around you from the classroom window. Better still, go out on as many field visits as possible – perhaps to a park, woodland, hedgerow, farm or pond. Observe, record and discuss signs of change in such things as the weather, leaves, flowers, signs of animals, birds and insects. [1a, 1b, 2a-c, 3a-f]
● *Make lists of 'signs of spring', 'signs of autumn' and so on. Decide with the children which of these can be measured, recorded or investigated in greater depth. Design and carry out appropriate investigations. [1a-c, 2a-c, 3a-f]
● *Go beyond what is immediately observable, for example, changing leaf colour on trees, signs of buds opening, morning frosts; ask the children to predict what further changes they may see and what effects on the world these changes may have. Test predictions wherever possible. [1a-c, 2a-c, 3a-f]
● *Make 'seasonal change' recording sheets (individually or on a class basis) with two columns. On the left-hand side, record observations – and on the right-hand side, try to explain why and/or how the change happened. [1c, 2a, 2b, 2c]
● As a result of field investigations and repeated observations, write accounts of some of the key characteristics of the season(s), explaining phenomena wher-

ever possible. [3a, 3c, 3d, 3e, 3f]
● Simplify the above if necessary by suggesting that the children draw or paint pictures of seasonal indicators, and beneath write a caption stating what is depicted and a simple explanation. [3a, 3c, 3f]

(NOTE: The above are relevant to many other activities suggested throughout the topic.)

**Life processes and living things**
● *Identify parts of flowering plants and trees visible in different seasons, helping children to appreciate change through the seasons. [1b, 1c]
● Talk and write about how humans respond to the changing seasons (for example, by wearing different clothes, turning heating on or off) and why various changes are made. [1b, 2f]
● *Do further investigations of plant responses to seasonal change. Introduce concepts such as deciduous, evergreen, annual, perennial. [1a-c, 5a-b]
● *Pursue research on how animals, birds and insects respond to seasonal change. Do sub-topics on such topics as hibernation, migration, life-cycles. [1a-b, 4b, 5a-b]

**Physical processes**
● *Discuss and investigate changing hours of daylight as the seasons go by. Make models of the Earth, Sun and Moon in order to provide an explanation of how and why the seasons occur. [3a-b]

# ENGLISH

**Speaking and listening**
● Talk about observations and feelings related to the season(s) you are studying. Ask the children to describe their personal thoughts and reflections: what they like about the season; what they least like about it; which is their favourite season, and why. [1a-d, 2a-b, 3a-b]
● Organise a class debate on one or more of the seasons, asking children to put forward reasons why this is the best/least favourite season of the year. [1a-d, 2a-b, 3a-b]

● Read aloud stories, poems and rhymes with a seasonal theme for the children to listen to and discuss. [1a-d, 2a-b, 3a-b]

**Reading**
● Provide a range of simple reading material for the learning of basic vocabulary associated with the seasons: perhaps a display of pictures/posters bearing the name of the season and key words beneath. [1b, 1c, 2a, 2b, 2d]

• Set up a reading corner with reference books, poems, rhymes and stories about the season(s) you are studying for the children to access freely. [1a-d, 2a-d, 3]

• Devise specific questions about the season(s), perhaps relating to field observations, in order for the children to select and use appropriate information sources and reference books. [1b, 1c, 2a, 2b, 2d, 3]

### Writing
• Help the children to write labels (simple or complex) for classroom displays relating to objects collected to represent the seasons (autumn fruits, summer flowers, winter twigs, etc.) [1a-c, 2a-e, 3a-b]

• Encourage the writing of individual or class illustrated poems or rhymes about the season(s). [1a-c, 2a-e, 3a-b]

• Help the children to compile an illustrated dictionary of the season(s) you are studying. Let them use this as a reference work throughout the topic. [1a-c, 2a-e, 3]

• Write stories about the seasons – telling of real events or imaginative scenarios, such as 'The Year It Snowed In Summer', 'The Strangest Winter', and so on. [1a-c, 2a-e, 3a-b]

• Produce a range of writing in individual work books and for display purposes, recording and reflecting on field observations and investigations. [1a-c, 2a-e, 3a-b]

• Encourage personal reflective writing on such topics as 'The Most Beautiful Season'; 'I Love Summer because …', and so on. [1a-c, 2a-b, 3a-b]

• Display pictures, paintings, collages of the season(s) you are studying alongside key words written by the children which best describe the season. [1a-c, 2a-e, 3a-b]

# GEOGRAPHY

### Geographical skills and places
• Record weather observations throughout the season(s) you are studying. Relate to other observations of the natural world. [1a, 2, 3b]

• Use a globe and reference material to help children appreciate that the seasons are not the same in all locations in the world; for example, when it is winter in the UK it is summer in Australia and New Zealand. [1c, 2, 3c, 3f, 4, 5a-d]

• Following on from the above, research ways of life of people in countries where the seasons are very different from our own – for example, lands where Christmas is celebrated on the beach. [1c, 2, 3e, 3f, 4, 5a-d]

• Research aspects of life and the environment in places where there are no clearly demarcated seasons – i.e. lands close to the equator. [1c, 2, 3e, 3f, 4, 5a-d]

• Focus on a sub-topic of the seasons in one specific distant locality, for example, seasons of the Arctic. Compare with our own country. [1a-c, 2, 3e, 3f, 4, 5a-d]

# MATHEMATICS

### Using and applying mathematics
All activities below provide opportunities for using and applying mathematics.

• Use mathematics as an important and integral part of investigating the characteristics and the nature of the changing seasons; selecting materials and mathematics to use for each practical task, for example, calculating hours of daylight and darkness, measuring and recording details of the weather, counting birds and insects observed, and so on. [1a-b, 2a-d, 3a-d, 4a, 4b]

### Number
• Count animal, insect and bird species observed in the season(s) under consideration – compare counts with other seasons of the year. [1a, 1c, 1d, 1e, 2a-c, 3c, 3d, 3e, 5a-b]

• Discuss the seasons as a fraction of the whole year and devise number puzzles accordingly, for example, when spring and summer have gone, we have had (half) of the whole year; the season of autumn is (a quarter) of the year. [1a, 2c]

• Interpret data that has been collected on the seasons, for example, weather statistics, bird counts, flower counts. Record on graphs or other pictorial /statistical diagrams. [1f]

• Record information collected on an appropriate database, and access when required. [1f]

• Consider seasonal changes and events in the light of data obtained. Discuss and order them in terms of 'likelihood'. Talk about and justify such decisions. [1a, 1c, 1e, 1f, 4a, 5a-b]

# ART

### Investigating and making
• Make pictures, paintings and collages of the four seasons, based on direct experiences. Pay particular attention to texture, colour and general mood or 'feelings' of each season. Display results in groups of four, one for each season, to highlight the contrast.

- Encourage the children to experiment with mixing paint colours to achieve the most effective representation of seasonal tints – for example, autumn leaf colour change, delicate shades of green in springtime, and so on.
- Make seasonal needlecraft wall hangings: let each child or group of children embroider or sew using simple collage/appliqué techniques symbols of the seasons (such as conker, snowman, snowdrop, sun, snowflake, pumpkin, etc.) on to squares of material. Stick these together to form a colourful hanging.
- Make papier mâché models (as near as possible to scale) of the Earth, Sun and Moon, and suspend them from the ceiling as a demonstration of why the Earth has seasons.
- Provide the children with a series of pictures/images of the seasons, perhaps cut from magazines or tourist brochures. Let the children sort them into seasonal sets and then glue them in an aesthetically pleasing way to make a collage/montage for each season.
- Discuss the predominant 'colours' of each season. Do the children associate particular colours with each season? Print or paint pictures of the season(s), restricting the children to two or three selected colours. Talk about why certain colours are associated with particular times of year.

**Knowledge and understanding**
- Collect pictures/reproductions of the work of artists on seasonal themes; or take children to an art gallery to observe works of art. Discuss the colours and moods portrayed by these works. Consider whether dominant colours are similar to those discussed in the above activity.

## R.E. ▶

- Research special days and festivals that take place in each season of the year. Do sub-topics on the celebrations and significance of one or more of these. Find out whether they are of religious or pagan origins, and if the former, more about the religion to which they belong.

## MUSIC ▶

**Performing and composing**
- Make sounds on a variety of instruments to represent feelings about the seasons. Perhaps the children could compose their own 'Symphony of the Seasons', or more simply, a tune for each season of the year. Record their compositions and let others listen, perhaps in the context of a school assembly.
- Learn to play and sing a variety of published songs and hymns about the seasons.

**Listening and appraising**
- Listen to music that has been composed about the seasons – ranging from simple songs to classical pieces such as Vivaldi's 'Four Seasons'. Discuss how sounds and rhythms are used to achieve particular effects.

**Blueprints links**
**Art Key Stage 1:** activities 71, 178, 201; **Art Resource Bank:** copymasters 61–2; **Assemblies 5–8:** photocopiable assemblies for each season; **Christmas Art and Craft:** activities for Christmas; **Early Years Songs and Rhymes:** many songs and rhymes on the seasons; **Easter:** many activities and copymasters on Spring; **Environmental Education Key Stage 1:** topic on weather; **Festivals:** different festivals covered at different seasons; **Geography Key Stage 1:** many activities on weather and seasons and copymasters; **History Key Stage 1:** topic on celebrations contains activities and copymasters on seasonal celebrations in history; **Infant Geography Resource Bank:** section on weather and climate, copymasters 91–96; **Infant Teacher's Resource Bank:** copymasters 47–50 (pictures of the four seasons), 51–57; **Poetry Book:** section on seasons, copymasters 25–8; **Religious Education Key Stage 1:** copymasters 77–79; **Science Key Stage 1:** activities and copymasters in Life processes and living things and Physical processes; **Seasonal Activities** complete book on the seasons; **Writing 5–8:** copymasters 10, 11, 16–20, 22–26, 28–30, 35, 36, 58.

# FARMS

## ENGLISH

- Discuss words and meanings associated with farms
- Discuss safety on a farm
- Talk about a farm visit
- Set up a farm reading corner
- Read stories and poems about farm life
- Make labels for samples and pictures
- Read 'The Country Code'
- Write about farm safety and behaviour
- Write farm words for display
- Do sentences completions
- Match pictures with labels
- Write factual accounts
- Write poems and stories about farm life

## GEOGRAPHY

- Follow a farm route
- Study farm plans
- Study aerial photographs
- Devise farm plans and maps
- Identify farming activities
- Consider location of farm buildings
- Study farming in UK and elsewhere
- Relate weather conditions to practices
- Interview a farmer
- Consider the importance of soil and water
- Identify landscape features
- Study farm buildings
- Discuss farming as a job
- Investigate farm and community links
- Discuss farm sizes.
- Find out about farm habitats and conservation

## ART

- Make crop prints
- Make pumpkin lanterns
- Make a farm frieze
- Make a model farm
- Construct a scarecrow
- Create a collage farm
- Model farm animals
- Study works of art
- Consider seasonal mood and colour

## ENVIRONMENTAL EDUCATION

- Discuss food chains and webs
- Consider what are 'pests'
- Discuss conservation and role of wildlife on farms
- Investigate how to deal with pests
- Debate controversial practices

## MATHEMATICS

- Undertake mathematical investigations
- Do animal leg calculations
- Do 'animal body' sums
- Practice compass directions

## HISTORY

- Study farming through the ages
- Make 'then and now' pictures
- Tell farming stories of the past
- Visit a museum of farming
- Interview someone about the past

## SCIENCE

- Classify plants and animals
- Study growth and life cycles
- Investigate basic needs of farm life
- Find out links between animals and crops
- Investigate farm habitats
- Observe and investigate farm activities
- Grow some crops

## MUSIC

- Sing farming songs
- Compose farm sounds and music

## ECONOMIC AND INDUSTRIAL UNDERSTANDING

- Consider farming as employment and a business

**IDEAS BANK**
General starting points: Suggestions for programmes of study of core and foundation subjects relating to topic, and links with cross-curricular themes and R.E.

**STARTING POINTS**
● Make a collection of pictures of farm animals, crops grown on farms and foods which derive from farms.
● Obtain an item(s) from a farm for close study in the classroom, e.g. a sheaf of corn, sample of sheep fleece, turnip, potatoes.

● Take the children on a visit to a farm. Decide whether this will be an arable farm, a livestock or a mixed farm. If possible, make a series of visits, either to one farm so that in-depth work can be undertaken and changes noted from visit to visit; or visit farms in each of the three categories mentioned above.
● Invite a farmer to come to school and talk to the class, in a structured interview situation.

# ENGLISH

**Speaking and listening**
● Brainstorm the word 'farm' – go around the class asking children to name items associated with farms – animals, plants, people, tasks, machines etc. Discuss answers. Help to reinforce the connection in the children's minds between people, animals, the land and food supply. [1a-c, 2a-b]
● Talk about the importance of safety on a farm. Ensure children respond to safety instructions when on a visit. [1c]
● After a visit, ask the children to talk individually about their favourite aspects of it, or to work in groups to prepare a presentation on some aspect of the visit. [1a-c, 2a-b]

**Reading**
● Set up a library corner of books relating to the topic – containing reference material, stories, poems and pictures about various farms, farming activities and farm life. Encourage the children to browse as well as respond to specific research and reading tasks. [1a-d, 2d]
● Talk about stories and poems read, discuss how farms and farmers depicted resemble or differ from farming scenes encountered by the children in real life. [1a-d, 2c]
● Make labels for farm samples or pictures in the classroom for the children to read. Let them match labels with appropriate picture or object. [1a-c]
● Help the children to read The Country Code – or write out a simplified, illustrated version of this for them to read. Discuss the content and importance of this. [1a-c, 2c]

**Writing**
● Write accounts of appropriate safety rules on a farm, or list of 'Do's' and 'Don'ts' to be adopted during a visit, e.g. 'Do close all gates' 'Don't drop litter', 'Don't run when you are near animals'. Link with learning of The Country Code with younger children – display pictures or symbols of such rules with accompanying simple phrases. (The learning of The Country Code and rules of safety are well worth while even if field visits are not being undertaken). [1a-c, 2a-b]
● Let the children write labels of basic farm words: names of animals, crops, machines etc. Match labels with pictures (cut from magazines or painted by the children). [1a-c]
● Provide simple beginnings of sentences that the children can complete with words or simple phrases, e.g. 'The names of some of the vegetables we get from a farm are ...' 'A farmer with cows has lots of jobs to do such as ...' [1a-c]
● Provide a series of pictures of farm animals and a parallel series of pictures of foods which animals eat (e.g. rye grass, wheat, barley, oats, mangold, clover, turnip, kale, sugar beet, maize). At a simple level, ask children to match animal labels with foods; older children can write complete sentences about what each animal might eat. [1a-c]
● Write factual accounts of such things as 'Things we can eat from a farm', 'A day (or year) in the life of a farmer', 'At home on the farm', 'All good things a cow (or any other farm animal) can give us', 'Food from the farm'. [1a-c, 2a-b]
● Ask the children to write creative stories and poems about animals and farm life, with ideas deriving from scenes observed or pure imagination. [1a-c, 2a-b]

# GEOGRAPHY

**Geographical skills**
● Follow a route around a farm, or study plans of a farm. [2, 3a-c, 3e]
● If possible, obtain aerial or other photographs of a farm. Use alongside plans or maps to identify and talk about features (fields, buildings, hedgerows, ponds, etc.). [2, 3b-f]

● Devise plans or maps of real or imaginary farms for the children to interpret, giving practice in identifying features, the use of scale, keys, etc. [2, 3d-e]

**Places and themes**
● Identify specific activities carried out by local farmers e.g. dairy farmers, poultry rearing, etc. [4, 5b-d]

- Help the children to understand why particular farm buildings and practices are located where they are. [5d]
- Compare farming practices of the local area with those of other places in the UK and beyond. [4, 5b]
- Undertake a sub-topic on farming around the world; find out how weather conditions help to determine the nature of farming practices in contrasting locations. Discuss why we cannot grow all crops in the UK. [5a-d]
- Interview a local farmer. Ask specific questions to help find out how weather in different seasons affects farmers' tasks, and how the farmer's year is largely dependent upon the seasons. [5c]
- Consider the importance of soil to the farmer, and the dependence of farming practices on the availability of water in the environment. (5a-b)
- Identify landscape features on a farm (by a visit or studying a plan or map). Discuss how particular features (e.g. hill, valley, stream, pond) affect the farmer's work. [5a-b]
- Make a particular study of farm buildings. Discuss their variety and purposes for which they are used (e.g.

farm house, milking parlour, machinery storage shed, silo). [5d]
- Help the children to appreciate that farming is a very important job, and that some people earn their living in this way. Discuss the work and importance of farmers. Compare and contrast with other types of employment. [5a-d]
- Investigate how farms operate in the local community and economy – find out what goods they supply and where they are marketed.
- Discuss sizes of various farms; if possible, visit farms of various sizes. Discuss why some farming practices take up more space than others. Discuss why, for example, modern arable fields (which use combine harvesters) are much larger than fields bounded by hedgerows in days gone by. [5d]
- Discuss the importance of farm habitats for conservation, e.g. hedgerows and ponds are important homes for wildlife. Help the children to appreciate how changes in farming practices over the years, e.g. hedgerow removal, have affected life in the country-side. [5a-c]

# SCIENCE

### Experimental and investigative science
- Visit a farm. Observe common farming activities and practices (e.g. cows being milked, animals being fed, crops being watered and harvested). [2a-b]
- If a series of visits is possible, predict and observe sequential happenings and changes in animals and crops through time. [2a-c]
- Grow some farm crops: seeds of grains such as wheat can be germinated in pots in the classroom. Let the children set up experimental conditions to investigate light conditions. Identify the factors critical for growth; warmth, water, space and nutrition from the soil. [1a-c, 2a-c]
- Grow seeds in different types and quantities of soil (e.g. using specially prepared seed compost, soil from the garden, sand, etc.). Discuss the nature and content of soil; its texture, and why it is crucial for a farmer. Plan fair tests to investigate plant growth in various types of soil. [1a-c, 2a-c]

### Life processes and living things
- Learn basic farm vocabulary including animal and plant names. Help the children sort these into sets (e.g.

animals/plants, root crops/cereal crops) and to match names of animal parents with their young (e.g. cow, calf; hen, chick; ewe, lamb). [4b]
- Talk and investigate more about how young animals grow and develop and about life patterns and cycles on a farm. Relate to animals on a farm, and whether they are kept to maturity or not. [1b]
- Find out more about how plants (crops) grow and their basic needs, including light. [3a-c]
- Help children to discover and appreciate the basic link between animals and food crops on a farm. Pose key questions for investigation, e.g. which crops are given to feed animals and which are grown for human consumption? [5a]
- Write about conditions necessary to sustain the forms of life on the farm you are studying, e.g. food, water. shelter, warmth, light. (1b, 3a, 5a)
- Undertake a sub-topic on 'habitats of the farm'. Perhaps children could be divided into groups, each group to focus on a particular habitat (e.g. fields, trees, ponds, walls, buildings, hedgerows, streams) and find out what/who lives there, and what conditions for life and growth are like. [5a]

# MATHEMATICS

### Using and applying mathematics
- Select specific farm-based tasks and problems to investigate and select the materials and mathematics to use for practical tasks, e.g. weighing/measuring animals, plants or animals' food; measuring buildings or fields. [1a, 2a-d, 3d]

### Number
- With a very young child, count legs on various types of animals. Sort into sets, i.e. those with two legs, those with four. Undertake more complex tasks, such as calculating how many legs in a farmer's herd of cows. [1a, 1c, 2a-b, 3a-d, 4a-b]

- Investigate how much milk a cow produces each day. Ask the children how this compares with the amount they drink as a class in a day. Similar comparisons could be made with egg production and consumption. [1a, 1c, 4a-d]
- Make careful estimates and measurements of plant growth; either in the classroom or on a series of visits to a farm. Compare growth of different plants in the same crop, or of different types of plant. [1a, 1c, 4a-d]
- Pose some interesting questions based on farm animal bodies, which are a fascinating source of mathematics on number e.g. How many stomachs does a cow have? How many would four cows have? How many toes do two hens have? [1a, 1c, 4a-d]

**Shape, space and measures**
- Whilst on a farm visit practise using the compass, and help children to locate fields, buildings and other objects in relation to each other by using the points of the compass [3a-b]

# ENVIRONMENTAL EDUCATION

- Discuss 'Who eats who?' on the farm. This will help children to understand food chains and that the food preferences/needs of some creatures are more hindrance than help to a farmer. Introduce the concept of pests on a farm; seed-eating birds; crop-eating slugs.
- Link the above activity to the key concept of conservation. Organise a class debate on whether all creatures should be encouraged to live on a farm, irrespective of whether they destroy others which are apparently more valuable. Consider the place, for example, of wild animals, birds and insects in farm habitats.
- Find out more about which farm habitats in particular encourage wildlife and conservation.
- Find out more about how farmers can deal with unwanted pests, causing as little damage as possible to other living things and the environment.
- Organise a class debate on one or more controversial aspects of farming, e.g. keeping battery hens.

# HISTORY

**Range and depth of historical knowledge and understanding**
- Investigate objects which represent farming in days gone by, e.g. find pictures of early ploughs and milking machinery. Place objects or pictures relating to a particular activity in chronological order. Talk about how farming activities have changed through time. [1a-b, 2a-c]
- Make 'then and now' pictures, e.g. a pair of pictures of harvest time in medieval times and harvest time today; milking time in the Victorian era, milking time today; ploughing in Saxon times, ploughing today. Compare and contrast the pictures and talk about why activities and farming scenes have changed through time. [1a-b, 2a-c]
- Tell the children stories about farming activities of the past, e.g. corn dolly making as an old pagan harvest-time custom. Discuss such stories and place their events in sequence. Compare their content with present day activities. [1a-b, 2a-c]

**Historical enquiry**
- Visit a museum of agriculture, or general museum which has agricultural artefacts. Use as a basis for discussion and further research. [4a-b]
- If there is a suitable person in the locality, invite an 'elderly' farmer to come and talk to the children about how farming has changed during his or her lifetime. Help children to appreciate in this way that people can be a crucial source of information about the past. (4a-b)

# ART

**Investigating and making**
- Make prints and patterns using farming products. Ears of wheat and barley print well on to material. Roots and tubers, including potatoes, carrots and turnips, can be cut into shapes and used for printing patterns and pictures on to paper or material.
- If the topic is being conducted in autumn time, make pumpkin lanterns. Hollow out a pumpkin, cut a face on the outside skin, and place a night light inside. Use the flesh for cookery activities.
- Make a large wall frieze of a farm you have visited or read about. Depict and label all key buildings and fields, showing what is grown or reared.
- Make a model farm – again this could be of a real or imaginary place. Construct the buildings out of cardboard which can then be organised on to a painted base plan (link with geography activities).
- Make a classroom scarecrow. A life-sized model made with broomsticks and old clothes could stand in front of a model or wall frieze. Use this as a focal point for creative writing and drama.
- Create a collage farm on the classroom wall. Indi-

viduals or groups could work on different aspects of this; use scraps of wool collected from hedgerows, off-cuts of leather, leaves and twigs, real features collected on walls, and seeds or stems of cereal crops if these can be obtained.
- Make models of farm animals from card or papier mâché; Display on your model farm or in front of a frieze.

### Knowledge and understanding
- Study the work of artists who have depicted farming scenes of past and present times. This activity can relate to history by using works of art as a source of information about farming in the past. Discuss not only the content of pictures, but also the colours and mood portrayed.
- Following on from the above, observe agriculture paintings set in the various seasons and let children assess the dominant colours (if any) of each season on the land. Discuss why, for example, autumnal pictures are often in shades of gold; spring pictures in green. This can be linked to science activities on seasonal changes on a farm.

# MUSIC ▶

### Performing and composing
- Teach the children well-known rhymes, songs and hymns about farms and farm life, e.g. 'Old MacDonald Had A Farm', 'The Farmer Works In The Fields All Day', 'Baa Baa Black Sheep'.
- Make farming sounds and compose your own 'farming music'. Use whatever instruments you have available to invent sounds that represent animal noises and movements.

# ECONOMIC AND INDUSTRIAL UNDERSTANDING ▶

### Economic and industrial understanding
- Help the children to appreciate basic concepts relating to farming and the world of work, e.g. that a farm is a place of employment; that a farmer breeds and feeds animals and helps crops to grow so that this enterprise provides food for people and other living things. This could well be begun by interviewing a farmer and asking him or her what happens to the farm's products. Plot their route to market (relate to geography activities). Find out who buys them and for what purposes.

### Blueprints links
**Assemblies 5–8:** photocopiable assembly on food; **Early Years Songs and Rhymes:** many songs and rhymes on farming and food; **Environmental Education Key Stage 1:** complete topics on farms and food; **Festivals:** topic on harvest and thanksgiving; **Geography Key Stage 1:** many activities and copymasters 1, 3, 20, 41, 66, 112, 113, 116; **History Key Stage 1:** topic on going to work contains activities and copymasters on farms in history; **Infant Geography Resource Bank:** copymasters 41–52 (producing milk, wool, strawberries); **Infant Teacher's Resource Bank:** copymasters 106–108 (food from farms), 136 (farm animals); **Religious Education Key Stage 1:** copymaster 23; **Seasonal Activities:** Spring 8; Autumn 10; **Second Key Stage 1 Topics Book:** complete topic on food and farming with copymasters; **Technology Key Stage 1:** many activities and copymasters.

# TOYS

## ENGLISH

- Study and discuss toys brought into school
- Read and tell stories and poems about toys
- Investigate favourite toys
- Write/draw imaginary stories and poems about toys
- Record details of scientific investigations
- Label classroom displays and write informative captions
- Write factually about school visit(s), history of toys and other relevant information

## MATHEMATICS

- Predict outcome of investigations
- Test predictions
- Measure and weigh any items being tested
- Talk about creating a toy shop
- Compare and order selected toys
- Look at shapes used for making toys
- Sort toys into sets
- Investigate probability
- Represent data pictorially and on a database

## GEOGRAPHY

- Study the Roamer and relate to points of a compass
- Investigate where toys are made
- Find out the origins of various materials

## HISTORY

- Study toys over a period of time
- Visit a toy museum or similar
- Find out more about toys of the past
- Study pictures, books and other artefacts
- Learn the history of some of the toys
- Discuss toys today and the makeshift toys of poor children in Victorian times

## ART

- Collect pictures, etc. of modern and historical toys
- Make a variety of toy pictures
- Design and make a wall frieze on toys
- Make toy mobiles
- Design and make puppets

## SCIENCE

- Investigate materials used in toymaking
- Study how toys move, speak, etc.
- Investigate old/broken toys
- Predict movement of toys
- Investigate surfaces used for moving toys
- Study materials and their properties
- Sort toys
- Test a selection of materials

## P.E. (Dance)

- Create a 'toy' dance using selected music or the 'toy symphony'

## MUSIC

- Use instruments to compose 'toy' music and/or a 'toy symphony'
- Learn a selection of songs about toys
- Listen to toys which make sounds
- Listen to selected pieces of music by well-known composers

## DESIGN AND TECHNOLOGY

- Discuss the need for making toys for a shop
- Design, plan, make and evaluate a working toy model
- Learn to use the Roamer
- Structure a simple database

31

**IDEAS BANK**
General starting points: Suggestions for programmes of study of core and foundation subjects relating to topic, and links with cross-curricular themes and R.E.

**STARTING POINTS**
● Bring a few toys into school, including if possible one or two of your own – especially any which have a story attached to them! Tell the children that they will be looking at many different kinds of toys over the next

few weeks, and ask them to bring some of their own toys into school – avoiding toys which may be very expensive or easily broken. Explain that it would be interesting to have a toy display in the classroom, and that their help is essential for this.
● Plan a visit to a general museum or a museum of childhood to look at toys of bygone days. Perhaps a corner of the classroom exhibition could be devoted to 'toys from the past'.
● Tell or read stories involving a toy or toys, for example, *The Tin Soldier* or *Pinocchio*.

# ENGLISH

**Speaking and listening**
● As a class, talk about all the toys when they are brought in. Let the children discuss their favourite toys and encourage them to give reasons for their choice. [1a-d, 2a-b, 3a-b]
● Let the children work in pairs or small groups to plan an imaginary story about a toy of their choice. When they are ready, let them tell their stories to the rest of the class. [1a-d, 2a-b, 3a-b]

**Reading**
● Discuss the content of some of the stories told/read to the children. [1a, 1c, 1d, 2c, 3]
● Tell the children the beginning of a real or imaginary story relating to toys, ask them to predict what

might happen next and how they think the story will end. The children could work in pairs or small groups and draw or write their version of the story. Let them tell/read these to the rest of the class. [1a, 1c, 2c, 3]

**Writing**
● Let the children write imaginary stories about a toy or toys, for example, 'The Magical Toyshop', 'Teddy's Exciting Day', 'The Dinosaur That Began To Grow', and so on. [1a-c, 2a-e, 3a-b]
● Help the children to record details of any scientific investigations. [1a-c, 2a-e, 3a-b]
● Let the children make labels and write informative captions about their classroom display. [1a-c, 2a-e, 3a-b]

# SCIENCE

**Experimental and investigative science**
All activities below provide opportunities for experimental and investigative science.
● Both individually and as a class, discuss and look closely at the various materials used in the making of the toys brought in for display. [2a, 3c, 3d, 3e, 3f]
● Investigate the different methods used to make the toys move, speak or make sounds. Some old, broken toys could be used to show hidden 'works'. [1a-c, 2a, 2b, 3a, 3c, 3d, 3e, 3f]
● Let the children predict which toys capable of movement will travel the greater distance, or which will travel fastest. Test the outcome of their predictions. [1a-c, 2a-c, 3a-f]
● Discuss whether the surface a toy car travels on will affect its speed, and let the children experiment using different surfaces (for example, rough/smooth). Mark the distance that each car travels and discuss findings

with the class. Help the children to record their findings in appropriate ways. [1a-c, 2a-c, 3a-f]

**Materials and their properties**
● Discuss with the children the properties of various materials used to make the toys on display – are they hard, soft, natural, synthetic; renewable or non-renewable, and so on? Talk about the implications of this. [1a, 1c, 1d, 1e, 2a-b]
● Ask the children to group all/some of the toys according to their observable features. [1b]
● Ask the children to help collect a variety of natural and synthetic materials that may be used to make toys. [1a-e, 2a-b]
● Working in groups, let the children test a selection of the above materials for heating/cooling/heat retention; melting/solidifying; floating/sinking, etc. Ask the children to record their findings. [2a-b]

# MATHEMATICS

## Using and applying mathematics

All activities below provide opportunities for using and applying mathematics.

● Let the children select the appropriate materials and mathematics to use for tasks when testing cars, recording findings, measuring activities etc. [1a-b, 2a-d, 3a-d, 4b]

● Discuss with the children any relevant investigations of toys and their possible outcomes. Let the children test their own predictions, discuss results and record their findings. [1a-b, 2a-d, 3a-d, 4b]

● With the whole class, talk about the various shapes used by the children when making model toys during technology activities. Use correct mathematical terms to describe two-dimensional shapes and three-dimensional objects used by the children in the making of their toys. [2a-c]

## Number

● As a class, discuss the possibility of setting up a class toy shop. Help the children to assess what is required and also to construct and operate the shop. [1a, 1c, 1e, 2a-c, 3c, 3d, 4a, 4b, 5a]

● Let the children sort appropriate toys into sets. [5a]

● Help the children to construct class/individual graphs/diagrams to show which toys are most popular; the order of colour used for the cars, etc. [1e, 5b]

● Design a simple data collection sheet for each child's favourite toy. Access the information in a database. [1e, 1f, 5b]

## Shape, space and measures

● Let groups of children take turns to compare and order selected toys without measuring them. [4a]

● Using appropriate toys and a Roamer, if available, discuss the ways in which equipment responds to signals and commands. Help the children to progress in giving a sequence of instructions to Roamer. [3a-b]

● Let the children work in groups to discuss, predict and test how far toy cars, lorries, etc. will travel on various surfaces (flat, inclined, rough, smooth, wet, dry). Tell the children to measure the distances travelled and record their findings. Give help and advice where necessary. Let the groups also measure the length of the cars being tested and weigh them. Do they think this is relevant to the cars' performance? [1a, 1c, 3a-b]

● With all the children, investigate probability; for example, it is certain that the car will travel down the slope but uncertain whether it will travel up. Encourage the children to use the appropriate mathematical language [3a, 3c, 4a-b]

# DESIGN AND TECHNOLOGY

## Design and technology capabilities

● With the class, and over a period of time, look at all the toys brought into school and discuss the different methods used to achieve movement. Ask the children whether they could make some additional toys themselves. Encourage a positive response. [1a-c, 2a-c]

● During class discussions, let the children talk about making a toyshop in the classroom. [1a-c, 2a-c]

## Designing skills

● Working in groups, let the children discuss/draw ideas for making their own individual toy. After discussion with teacher and others in the group, let the children choose one of their own ideas. [3a-f]

● Again working in small groups, ask children to discuss a class shop, to pool their ideas and ultimately – after class discussion – arrive at a class plan. [3a-f]

## Making skills, and knowledge and understanding

● Let the children select appropriate materials from as wide a range as possible, and with discussion and help where required, let them make their chosen toy. These can be very simple or, alternatively, moving toys after earlier discussion and investigation as to how various toys are made to move, for example, axles for wheels. [4a, 4b, 4c, 4d, 4e, 5a-g]

● With the class, let the children demonstrate the toys made. Encourage all the children to discuss each toy, the problems encountered, whether the design works well, etc. If several children make toys on wheels, let them race them and discuss the results. [1c, 4f, 5a-g]

## Information technology

● Structure a simple database and let the children use a computer for storing and retrieving information about their class toys. [1b, 2a-c, 3a, 5b]

# ART

**Investigating and making**

• Collect photographs and paintings/drawings of modern toys and toys from the past. Ask the children to help with this collection. Let them look for similarities and differences between these playthings.

• Using a wide range of materials and techniques, let the children design their own toy pictures.

• Hold class discussions about the creation of a wall frieze of 'Toyland', or some similar theme. Let the children give their ideas and after discussion help them to plan the chosen picture. Let all the children participate in the making of the frieze.

• Let the children design and make toy mobiles – teddy bears, rag dolls, cars and so on.

• Using a variety of materials, let the children make toy puppets and perhaps present simple plays, with selected grouping of the puppets.

# GEOGRAPHY

**Geographical skills and places**

• Let the children learn how to give instructions to the Roamer, making it move in a series of different directions. Relate this to the points of the compass. [1b, 2, 3c]

• With the class, investigate where a range of toys are made, who makes them and whether this is large or small scale manufacture. [1a-c, 2, 3e, 3f, 4, 5b]

• Help the children to investigate the origins of materials from which the toys are made. [1a-c, 2, 3e, 3f, 4, 5a]

# HISTORY

**Areas of study (Key Elements 1-5)**

• Take a range of toys from different eras (for example, the present day, 1950s, Edwardian or Victorian times). The selection could be actual artefacts or pictures of them, and might include dolls/dolls' houses, toy soldiers, spinning tops, board games, and so on. Let the children place them in chronological order. Use your own collection of toys, plus any brought in by the children. If some of the older toys are difficult to find, visit a toy museum. [1a-b]

• Help the children to find out more about toys of the past. Use pictures, books and other artefacts, and discuss how they can help us to answer questions about the past. [1b]

• Let the children read about the history of a particular toy, for example the football, or the teddy bear. Discuss what we can learn from this – not just about the toy, but about people and events through time. What was childhood like thirty, fifty, seventy or a hundred years ago? Emphasize the contrast between the lot of a modern child and that of, say, a Victorian child working in the factory, mine or chimney. [1b, 3]

# MUSIC

**Performing and composing**

• Let the children compose toy music patterns (for example, patterns for a teddy bear, a toy soldier, a rag doll and so on), using various instruments. Record these on large cards so that the other children can play the pattern, too.

• As a class, learn a selection of songs on the theme of toys perhaps including 'Teddy Bears' Picnic' (the most notable version is probably that recorded many years ago by Henry Hall and his Orchestra), 'Soldier, Soldier, Won't You Marry Me?', Tom Paxton's song 'The Marvellous Toy', and so on.

• Working in groups, ask the children to compose a 'toy symphony' using tuned or non-tuned instruments to make toy sounds.

**Listening and appraising**

• Collect and listen to toys which make sounds. Discuss with the children how these sounds could be replicated using musical instruments.

• Let the children listen to selected passages from well-known classical music with a toy theme, for example, Haydn's 'Toy Symphony' or Tchaikovsky's 'Nutcracker Suite'.

# P.E.

**Dance**
- Let the children work as a class to create a 'toy dance', moving as a variety of toys (for example, clock-work mice, dolls, marching soldiers, etc.) Perhaps their own 'toy symphony' could accompany this.

**Blueprints links**
**Art Key Stage 1:** many activities, copymasters 94, 95 (puppets); **Art Resource Bank:** copymasters 132–3; **Christmas Art and Craft:** toy making activities; **Early Years Songs and Rhymes:** many songs and rhymes on toys; **History Key Stage 1:** complete topic and many copymasters on toys in history; **Poetry Book:** section on games, copymasters 17–20; **Religious Education Key Stage 1:** copymasters 17–20; **Religious Education Key Stage 1:** copymasters 85; **Science Key Stage 1:** copymasters 75, 76, 91, 93; **Technology Key Stage 1:** many activities and copymasters; **Topics Key Stage 1:** complete topic on toys.

# SHOPS

## ENGLISH

- Discuss shopping in the local environment
- Read and tell holiday stories and poems with reference to shops/shopping
- Visit the local shopping area
- Write imaginary stories and poems about shops
- Label items and make posters for shops about selected exhibits and school outing
- Record details of scientific investigations
- Write factually about school visits and changes in shopping over the years

## GEOGRAPHY

- Make a simple route map
- Discuss local area and shopping facilities
- Investigate goods from other countries
- Arrange a display of imported goods
- Study construction of various local shops
- Talk about people employed by the retail industry

## ART

- Make pictures of favourite shops
- Design and make a shop/wall frieze
- Make advertising posters
- Use clay to make items for class shop
- Make wrapping paper
- Study posters, pictures and advertisements

## HEALTH EDUCATION

- Investigate the need for a healthy diet
- Study foods beneficial to good health
- Discuss health and safety laws in shops

## SHOPS

## MATHEMATICS

- Plan a class/school shop
- Measure ingredients if cake-making
- Learn about money/giving correct change, etc.
- Design wrapping paper
- Study shape and packaging
- Learn about tessellation
- Sort, compare and order objects in the class shop
- Represent data pictorially and on a database

## HISTORY

- Investigate changes in shops and shopping
- Study artefacts, pictures, etc. of shops and shopping in the past
- Discuss changes that have taken place
- Visit a local museum
- Study real/fictional stories about shops of the past

## DESIGN AND TECHNOLOGY

- Identify needs for a real cake shop and/or a class shop
- Design, plan, make and evaluate the required posters, labels, news sheets, etc.
- Make cakes for sale in class shop
- Use computer/DTP for creation of posters, advertising leaflets, etc.

## R.E.

- Discuss current changes in shopping and the law as it stands
- Study the work of selected charities which run shops

## SCIENCE

- Investigate natural and human-made materials
- Study hygiene in food shops
- Investigate conditions needed to sustain life
- Learn about human anatomy and how to take care of ourselves
- Investigate properties of selected materials
- Study some 'natural' foods
- Test selected foods for solubility, smell, etc.
- Discuss ingredients on food packaging

**IDEAS BANK**
General starting points: Suggestions for programmes of study of core and foundation subjects relating to topic, and links with cross-curricular themes and R.E.

**STARTING POINTS**
● Bring into school several items of shopping with their price labels and wrapping intact. Talk about where they came from and why they have price tags on them. Look at the way they are wrapped and discuss this, along with shopping in general.

● As a class, talk about the local shops – their variety and size, and whether the children go to other shops further away. If so, what kind of shops are they?
● If possible, arrange a visit to a local history museum to see shops from the past.
● Arrange for the children to visit the local shopping area and also, if possible, for them to be shown round one or two of the larger shops or stores. With Reception children a visit to one store may be sufficient.
● Have pictures, advertisements and photographs of local shops, as well as goods, to use as talking points.

# ENGLISH ▶

**Speaking and listening**
● Talk about the articles brought into class and the kind of shops they come from; discuss the different types of shops in the area. Let the children tell each other about their favourite shop(s) and the reason(s) for their selection. [1a-c]
● Read or tell appropriate stories and/or poems about shops and shopping. Talk about these with the children afterwards. [1a-c]
● Let the children work in pairs or groups to plan an imaginary story about a shop of their choice, for example, an old toy shop, a mysterious shop, or a sweet shop. Let the children tell their story to the rest of the class. [1a-d]

**Reading**
● Talk about the content and structure of stories about shops/shopping. With suggestions and help from the children, construct the beginning of an imaginary story about going shopping, and ask them individually or in pairs to predict the middle and end of the story. Let them tell their versions of the story to the other children. [1a, 1c, 1d, 2a, 2b, 2c, 3]

**Writing**
● Let the children write imaginary stories about shops and shopping, for example, 'The Magic Toy Shop', 'A Shopping Spree', 'A Surprise In A Doughnut', and so on. [1a-c, 2a-e, 3]
● Make labels and posters for shop(s). [1a-c, 2a-e, 3]
● Record details of science experiments, information obtained from visit(s) to shop(s) and changes in shopping habits over a period of time. [1a-c, 2a-e, 3]

# SCIENCE ▶

**Experimental and investigative science**
All activities below provide opportunities for experimental and investigative science.
● As a class, talk about and investigate some of the natural and man-made materials to be found in shop goods. Talk about what is meant by these descriptions and explain that many things, including clothing, are made from both kinds of materials. [1b, 1c, 2a, 3a, 4a-b]
● Discuss food shops and hygiene, the quality of food, and food additives. [1a, 1b, 1c, 2a-c, 3a, 4a-b, 5a-b]

**Life processes and living things**
● Talk to children about the conditions needed to sustain life, including food and water. [1a-b, 2b, 2c, 3a, 4b]
● Let the children talk about themselves and their anatomy, and encourage them to learn the main external parts of the body. Relate this to the need to take care of ourselves. This activity can be reinforced by appropriate worksheets. [1a, 2a-f, 4a-b]

**Materials and their properties**
● Look at a variety of materials, both natural and man-made, used in the manufacture of clothing. Test a selection of small pieces of material for water resistance, warmth, drying out, strength, and so on. Record tests and results. [1a-e, 2a-b]
● Investigate some 'natural foods' – flour, salt, sugar, dried peas, and so on. Do they smell, dissolve in water, melt in heat and so on. Let the children record any tests undertaken. [1a-e, 2a-b]
● Talk to the children about the 'ingredients' printed on packets and explain that they are set out in order of quantity contained within the food in the packet. Read one or two of these lists out loud and talk about the various ingredients. [1a-e, 2a-b]

# MATHEMATICS

### Using and applying mathematics
All activities below provide opportunities for using and applying mathematics.
- Let the children select the appropriate materials and mathematics for creating and operating a class or school shop, and recording statistics such as prices and sales figures. [1a-b, 2a-d, 3a-d, 4a-c]
- Plan and discuss individual tasks in the operation of the shop, as appropriate. [1a-b, 2c, 2d, 3c]

### Number
- Construct and operate a class/school shop. Help the children to price goods as realistically as possible, and encourage the correct use of money. [1a, 1c, 1d, 1e, 2a-c, 3c, 3d, 3e, 4a-d]
- Design wrapping paper for the class/school shop, using repeat patterns. [1a, 1c, 3a]
- Sort the objects in the class shop, and describe the criteria chosen. [1a, 1c, 5a]
- Plan graphs and/or other diagrams relating to the topic, for example, types of shops in the local area, the children's preferences for certain shops, favourite cakes, favourite sweets, etc. [1e, 5b]
- Construct a simple database for each child, based on, for example, favourite food/toy/garment/sweets etc. Let the children have practice with the computer in learning how to access and retrieve information. [1f, 5b]

### Shape, space and measures
- Discuss shapes in relation to packaging. Let the children have the experience of stacking/packing different three-dimensional objects/containers. Which items stack best? Why? Use correct mathematical terms to describe two-dimensional shapes and three-dimensional objects. [2a-c]
- Introduce the concept of tessellation, and let the children experiment with two-dimensional shapes. [2a-c]
- Compare and order objects in the class shop, without measuring. [4a]

# DESIGN AND TECHNOLOGY

### Design and technology capability
- As a class, discuss the possibility of a real cake shop, either for the class or the whole school. Plan for it to be open at certain times, for example, morning break for one day/week etc. Suggest proceeds from sales go to a chosen charity or School Fund. [1a-c, 2a-c]
- Talk about the site of the shop, time(s) when it might be open, how it would be set up, and so on. [1a, 1b, 2a-c]
- Also talk about the possibility of a more permanent 'corner store' in the classroom which the children can use for the duration of the topic. Ask the children to bring in clean empty cartons/containers, greetings cards, newspapers/magazines/comics and other items to 'sell'. [1b, 2a-c]

### Designing skills
- Talk about the class shop, where it will be situated, what to sell, and so on. [3a-f]
- Discuss posters/advertising for the cake shop. Talk about obtaining cakes for sale. Suggest that some can be made in class and, if the shop is to be accessible to other classes in the school, then other children need to be asked to make or bring in cakes for sale. [3a-f]
- Plan the price-fixing and sale of cakes. [3a-f]

### Making skills and knowledge and understanding
- Design poster(s), news sheet(s), price labels, etc. for goods in the class/school shop. [4a, 4b, 4c, 4d, 4e]
- Construct the shop, as planned. [4a, 4b, 4c, 4d, 4e, 5a-g]
- Let the children talk about their work and consider whether it meets all the requirements. [4f]
- Look at commercial advertisements (such as posters, hoardings, shopfront signs and so on) for local shops and discuss some of them together with posters, etc. made in class. [4f]

### Information technology
- Using the computer, printer and appropriate word processing or desk top publishing software (for example, 'Minnie' or 'Caxton'), let the children write and print out leaflets advertising the class/school shop. [1b, 2a-c, 3a, 3b]

# ART

### Investigating and making
- Help the children to use as many different materials and techniques as possible in their art work about shops.
- Suggest that the children create a picture showing their favourite shop window, and discuss how this might best be done – for example, types of collage, paint, felt-tip pens, etc.

- Help the children to make a wall frieze of, say, different shop frontages or perhaps one large shop window where three-dimensional effects could be incorporated.
- Ask the class to design and make posters advertising goods from relevant shop(s). Perhaps some of these can be put up around school if a school shop is planned.
- Use clay, Play-Doh™, etc. to make imitation food/sweets for the class shop.
- Design and make wrapping paper, some with repeat patterns and two-dimensional shapes for the class shop.

**Knowledge and understanding**
- During the topic, let the children look at and discuss a range of posters and other advertisements in magazines, newspapers, etc.
- Try to collect some pictures of shops/markets and talk about them. Discuss why there are not many paintings of shops. Can the children suggest why?
- Talk about the children's own work, discussing such issues as why particular colours and media are more effective than others.

# GEOGRAPHY ▶

**Geographical skills and places**
- Help the children to follow a simple map of their route to the shops. Later, let them draw/write on the map some of the interesting features they passed en route – for example, church, factory, swimming baths, park, and so on. [1a, 1b, 2, 3a, 3b, 3c, 3d]
- Discuss the local area and the proximity of shops/shopping centre. [1a, 1b, 2, 3a, 3b, 3c, 3d]
- If appropriate, compare shopping facilities in the local area with a contrasting site which may be fairly well-known to the children, for example, a small town or a large city nearby. [1a-c, 2, 3a-f, 4, 5b, 5d]
- Collect and display goods from different parts of the world (including Great Britain) which may be seen in our shops. Arrange these items in sets, and label each country of origin. Let the children find these countries on the globe. [1a-c, 2, 3e, 3f]

- Discuss different types of shops in the locality – their size and where they are situated. Are the shops purpose-built? (Sometimes a house is converted into a shop). Do any have car parks? If so, discuss why. [1a, 1b, 2, 3a, 3b, 3c, 4, 5a, 5d]
- Talk about the people whose work is connected with shops – for example, shop assistants, cleaners, transport drivers, window cleaners, etc. [1a, 1b, 2, 3a, 3b, 3c, 4, 5a, 5c]

**Thematic study**
- Talk to the children about the sites of shops – are new shops being built in the local area? Would they like to see changes to the local shops/shopping area? If so, what would they like changed? [6a-c]

# HISTORY ▶

**Areas of study (Key Elements 1-5)**
- Talk with the children about the changes in shops and shopping over a period of time. Perhaps an elderly person could be invited into school to talk about what shops were like when s/he was young. Encourage the children to ask grandparents and perhaps older neighbours about shopping in the past, and to tell the class about any interesting facts they have discovered. [1a-b]
- Look at photographs, pictures and books about shops nowadays and those of, say, 50-100 years ago. Collect artefacts from the past and place in approximate chronological order in front of an appropriate time-line. [1a-b]

- Discuss the many changes in shops and shopping habits over recent years. [1a]
- Arrange a class visit to a local museum if it contains a shop or shops set out as they would have appeared in the past. [1a-b]
- Let the children listen to real stories about shopping now and in the past, as told perhaps by the teacher, a former shopkeeper or a visitor to the school. Read or tell fictional stories and talk about the differences between the two kinds of story. [1a-b]
- Let the children study books, pictures and other artefacts (such as 'old', pre-decimal coinage) connected with the theme of shops and shopping. Discuss what can be deduced from these items. [1a-b]

# R.E.

- Discuss the changes currently taking place in shopping, for example, longer hours, Sunday shopping, travelling greater distances to shops and the growth of hypermarkets. Let the children give their views about these changes, after talking about all aspects.
- If proceeds from a cake shop are to be donated to a charity, talk about this with the children. If possible, let them make suggestions as to which charity should be helped. Consider the work of various local and/or national charities so that the children can make an informed choice of recipient.

# HEALTH EDUCATION

- Talk about food and the importance of eating a balanced diet to ensure good health. Discuss various foods which are considered good or bad.
- Tell the children about health and safety laws which shops have to obey. Discuss some of these regulations – such as food hygiene, mopping up spillages, safe trolleys and so on – with the children.

**Blueprints links**
**Geography Key Stage 1:** copymaster 7 (street survey), 9 (shop survey), 32, 33, 38 (going shopping), 47, 81–3 (shops and services); **History Key Stage 1:** complete topic and copymasters on money and shops in history; **Writing Book:** copymaster 1; **Infant Geography Resource Bank:** copymaster 52 (fruit and vegetable shop); **Technology Key Stage 1:** many activities and copymasters.

# HOLIDAYS

## ENGLISH

- Talk about holidays
- Read and tell holiday stories and poems
- Investigate the meaning of 'holiday'
- Discuss holidays at home
- Write real and imaginary holiday stories
- Label classroom displays and write factually about selected exhibits and school outings
- Record details of scientific investigations

## R.E.

- Discuss reasons why many people cannot go on holiday
- Talk about organised aid to people in need

## GEOGRAPHY

- Pinpoint holiday destinations on maps
- Investigate weather, scenery, food and so on
- Discuss reasons for holidays
- Find out about methods of travel
- Talk about the local area as a holiday resort

## ART

- Make holiday pictures
- Design and make a holiday frieze
- Make models for a holiday theme park or similar
- Examine holiday pictures, photographs etc.
- Establish a classroom 'art gallery'

## MUSIC

- Use instruments to make 'travel' sounds and compose 'travel' music
- Learn some holiday songs
- Compose holiday music
- Listen to selected pieces of music by well-known composers

## HOLIDAYS

## MATHEMATICS

- Use appropriate map to plot holiday journeys and estimate distances
- Learn about the 4/8 points of the compass
- Sort a collection of holiday postcards
- Represent data pictorially and on a database

## HISTORY

- Write or talk about holiday experiences
- Investigate holidays in the past and discuss changes
- Listen to personal experiences of holidays of, say, fifty years ago
- Examine evidence of holidays in the past from paintings, etc.
- Arrange a 'holiday' day out
- Write about the school outing and compare individual reports of the day

## DESIGN AND TECHNOLOGY

- Study the local area and assess any need for improved holiday facilities
- Design, plan, make and evaluate a model play/theme park
- Publish a holiday news sheet
- Construct simple database for storage and retrieval of holiday data

## P.E.

- Play holiday games
- Invent new games to play

## SCIENCE

- Collect holiday memorabilia including shells and stones
- Find out about sea water and fresh water
- Investigate differences and similarities between coast, country, town, and so on
- Discuss wildlife in respective areas
- Investigate floating and sinking
- Learn about tides and water forces

## IDEAS BANK
General starting points: Suggestions for programmes of study of core and foundation subjects relating to topic, and links with cross-curricular themes and R.E.

## STARTING POINTS
- Gather a selection of postcards together from various holiday resorts and give the children the opportunity to study them. The children could try to find the resorts in an atlas, or possibly sort them into sets. Ask them to bring more postcards from home to add to the collection.

- Talk about holidays and the children's personal experiences.
- Have pictures/books relating to holidays on display in the classroom, together with a few items such as shells, stones and gift-shop souvenirs to stimulate interest. Ask the children to bring in similar items from home and begin to set up a display area.
- Arrange a visit to a local holiday attraction such as a Safari Park, Botanical Gardens or some other popular site in the locality. Tell the children it's a 'holiday day.' Try to plan this activity as a whole day out, including a picnic lunch and a visit to a shop where the children may purchase inexpensive souvenirs.

# ENGLISH ▶

### Speaking and listening
- Talk about holidays in general, and the children's individual experiences. Encourage children to talk about a stay-at-home holiday, as some may not have had the good fortune to have a holiday away from home. Ensure that the stay-at-home holiday is not regarded as an inferior or second-rate holiday in any way: emphasise the importance of just having time to relax, away from day-to-day school work. Let children discuss their favourite holiday activities and places, and encourage them to give reasons for their choice. [1a-d, 2a-b, 3a-b]
- Let the children work in pairs/small groups to plan an imaginary story about a holiday adventure. When ready, let them tell their stories to the rest of the class. [1a-d, 2a-b, 3a-b]
- Tell or read holiday stories/poems to the class and talk about them afterwards. If possible, include a story about a holiday at home and/or a day out, such as 'A Gift From Winklesea' by Helen Cresswell. [1a-d, 2a-b, 3a-b]

### Reading
- After reading holiday poems and stories to the class, discuss their contents and structure, the sequence of events and so on. [1a, 1c, 1d, 2a-d, 3]
- Tell children the beginning of a real or imaginary story about a holiday and let them predict how the story might continue and end. [1a,1c,1d,2a-d,3]

### Writing
- Ask children to write imaginary stories about holidays. Look for evidence of structure/punctuation, etc. if applicable. [1a-c,2a-e,3a-b]
- Record details of any science experiments carried out on the theme of holidays. [1a-c, 2a-e, 3a-b]
- Label any classroom holiday display and write informative captions about selected exhibits. [1a-c, 2a-e, 3a-b]
- Write factual accounts of any school day out, and of any individual holiday experience. [1a-c, 2a-e, 3a-b]

# SCIENCE ▶

### Experimental and investigative science
All activities marked with an asterisk below provide opportunities for experimental and investigative science.
- * Look at objects such as shells, stones, etc. and talk about where they might be found in sea or other water, for example, floating or on the sea bed. Extend this discussion to other appropriate objects. Discuss and demonstrate the difference between sea water and fresh water. [1a, 1b, 1c, 2a-b, 3a, 4a-b, 5a-b]

### Life processes and living things
- Talk to the children about similarities and differences between coast, country and town. Discuss the wildlife that might be found in the respective areas. [1b, 4b, 5a-b]

### Materials and their properties
- * Investigate floating/sinking using objects from the classroom holiday collection and others, if appropriate.[1a-e,2a]
- * Discuss water/sea water (salt) and its holiday uses. Talk about tides and their effects upon both sea and shore. [1a-e, 2b]

### Physical processes
- * Talk about the force of water, waves, currents, tides. [2a-d]

# MATHEMATICS

## Using and applying mathematics
All activities below provide opportunities for using and applying mathematics.

## Number
● Let children select appropriate materials and mathematics for planning graphs/diagrams to record information relating to the holiday theme. This can be done individually, in pairs or in a small group. Discuss plans and any problems.
● Let children plan graphs/diagrams to record chosen holiday information, for example, who holidayed at home/abroad etc., which children like a seaside/country winter/summer holiday best. [1e, 5b]

● Ask children to sort the collection of holiday postcards and describe the criteria chosen. [5a]
● Construct simple database(s) recording, for example, places and countries visited, favourite type of holiday, favourite holiday activity, etc. Let children practise the storage and retrieval of such information. [1f]

## Shape, space and measures
● Let children plot holiday journeys on suitable map(s). Estimate the longest/shortest journey in this country, and check estimates by measuring (time taken/distance travelled). [4a-b]

# DESIGN AND TECHNOLOGY

## Design and technology capability
● Discuss holidays at home and whether and how the local area could be improved to make a holiday at home more exciting. Collect ideas and select an appropriate one for development, possibly with models (for example, a Theme Park, a play area, etc.) [1a-c, 2a-c]

## Designing skills
● As a class, look at relevant pictures, including the children's own art work. Let them talk and plan their ideal play area, theme park etc. [3a-f]
● Working individually or in small groups, let children design one selected part of an overall model. Encourage children to exchange ideas, draw and plan them if desired, and eventually to select the most suitable design for making. [3a-f]
● Involve children in the planning and designing of a holiday wall frieze. [3a-f]

## Making skills and knowledge and understanding
● Have a wide range of materials available and let

children select the most suitable material(s) and make their chosen model. Work with the children giving help and advice where appropriate. Encourage discussion as work progresses. [4a, 4b, 4c, 4d, 4e, 5a-g]
● Let children make necessary items for the holiday frieze. [4a, 4b, 4c, 4d, 4e]
● Assemble individual models to make a complete unit or holiday site. Let children evaluate and discuss the end product of their efforts, with the teacher and each other. [4f, 5a-g]
● Discuss the frieze as it is created and implement any constructive changes suggested by the children. [4f, 5a-g]

## Information technology
● Construct simple database(s) for storage and retrieval of holiday data. [1b, 1c, 2b, 2c, 3a, 3b]
● Using appropriate hardware and software, let children create (and desk top publish?) a holiday newssheet, contributing items such as news, handy hints, holiday stories, poems, puzzles, pictures and so on. [1a-c, 2a-c, 3a-c]

# ART

## Investigating and making
● Encourage children to create their own holiday pictures, using a wide range of materials and techniques such as paint, colour-wash, crayon, collage, and so on.
● Talk to children about a wall frieze and let them all participate in its creation.
● Arrange a display of holiday souvenirs, both natural and man-made, and encourage children to use such items as shells, pebbles, etc. in their art work.
● Let children plan and make models for an ideal holiday attraction at home.

## Knowledge and understanding
● Encourage children to bring in pictures of holidays, not only of places where they have been themselves. Discuss the differences between photographs and other prints/pictures. Try to acquire some prints of holiday scenes painted by well-known artists, both nowadays and in the past. Talk about all of these pictures and compare their contents, colour, atmosphere, technique etc.
● Let children talk about their own work, expressing what they consider to be its strengths.
● Arrange a collection of holiday pictures in an 'art gallery' in the classroom.

# GEOGRAPHY

**Geographical skills and places**
● Study holiday journeys on map(s) and begin to use the 4/8 points of the compass to give directions. [1c, 2, 3c, 3d, 3e]
● Discuss holidays in the local area and other places in Great Britain and abroad. [1a-c, 2, 3a, 3e, 3f, 4, 5a-d]
● Pinpoint holiday destinations visited by the children on a large map of Great Britain, and/or a map of the world if appropriate. Let the children talk about their holidays, for example, the weather, scenery, countryside/city, food, activities, and so on. [1a, 1b, 1d, 1e, 2a, 2b, 2c, 3b, 3c, 3d, 3e, 3f]

**Geographical skills and thematic study**
● Discuss why people take a holiday. Why is this usually in the summer? Talk about the seasons and climates in other countries. [1a-c, 2, 3e, 3f]
● Discuss methods of travel that people might choose to facilitate their holiday, or use while on vacation. Can children suggest reasons for any preferred means of transport? [1a-c, 2b]
● Let the children give their views on the local area as a holiday resort. Has it a lot to offer? Can it be improved? If so, how? What do people want to see and do while on holiday? [1a, 1b, 2, 3a, 3b, 4, 6a-c]

# HISTORY

**Areas of study (Key Elements 1-5)**
● Let children write or tell their own story about a holiday experience or day out. Encourage them to sequence the events, helping to develop a sense of chronology. [1a]
● Talk about holidays nowadays, then ask children to talk to their grandparents and other known older people about the holidays they enjoyed when they were young. Talk about the differences between holidays then and now. Try to arrange for one or two willing senior citizens to come into school and talk to the class about holidays 50+ years ago. Brief any visitors beforehand and structure any questions that the children may wish to ask, so that the talk or interview has clear guidelines and purpose throughout. [1a, 1b]
● Look at old pictures, photographs, postcards and videotapes showing holidays in the past and talk about

the differences then and nowadays. The children may well be interested, for example, in comparing a Victorian or Edwardian beach scene, with its bathing huts and strange swimming costumes, to scenes at modern seaside resorts. It may even be possible to show the children some old 8mm cinefilm of bygone family holidays. [1a, 1b]
● After a school outing for the children, ask them to draw and write about their day. Discuss similarities and differences in a variety of individual reports of the day. [1a]

**Use of historical sources**
● After looking at the photographs, etc. of holidays in the past as mentioned above, ask the children to make observations about them. What can the children discover from the pictures? [1a-b]

# MUSIC

**Performing and composing**
● Discuss different methods of travel and let the children experiment with different instruments to convey walking, flying, train, coach etc.
● Learn appropriate holiday songs and let children select appropriate instruments as accompaniment. Repertoire might include 'Summer Holiday', 'The Sun Has Got His Hat On', 'I Do Like To Be Beside The Seaside', and so on.
● Encourage children to compose their own holiday music and to record it. Suggest sounds of the sea or water music, or perhaps a story theme such as leaving home, paddling in the sea, falling asleep in the sun, returning home. Let the children play and record their music, and discuss it with the class.

**Listening and appraising**
● Select passages of music for children to listen to, including some from other countries (Spain, Greece, Hawaii, et.) and pieces such as 'Holiday For Strings', 'Coronation Scot', 'By A Sleepy Lagoon' (theme music for the long-running radio programme 'Desert Island Discs'), and so on. Talk about each piece of music and the instruments used, the rhythms within the piece, its mood and associations, etc. Encourage the children to suggest music worth listening to and perhaps bring in records/tapes of their own.

# P.E.

**Games**
● Discuss holiday games and use a variety of appropriate equipment to practise skills and play various games.

● Let children make up new games, individually or with a partner; show the game(s) to other children, explaining the aims and rules of the game.

# R.E.

● Talk about countries where most children cannot go on holiday because of poverty/famine/wars, etc. Let the class discuss this. Many will have watched TV programmes and seen the poverty and other problems which exist in the world. Discuss the different ways people are trying to help, some giving their lives to get medical supplies, food and clothing to those in need.

# HEALTH EDUCATION

**Health education**
● Discuss keeping healthy and safe whilst on holiday. Stress the need for care when near water or actually swimming. Ask the children to suggest safe places in which to play, and contrast this with dangerous places such as busy roads, near railway lines, cliff edges and so on. Talk about the dangers of too much sun, and ways of protecting ourselves from harm.

**Blueprints links**
**Assemblies 5–8:** Photocopiable assembly on colour; **Christmas Key Stage 1:** book on Christmas; **Distant Places:** many activities about holidays in six different countries; **Early Years Songs and Rhymes:** pages 22, 61, 66; **Festivals:** ten festivals covered, many copymasters; **Geography Key Stage 1:** copymaster 100 (holiday journeys); **History Key Stage 1:** topic and copymasters on seaside holidays in history; **Infant Geography Resource Bank:** copymasters 11–15 (seaside town); **Writing 5–8:** many related copymasters; **Seasonal Activities:** Summer copymasters 4, 6, 13, Summer template 3; **Technology Key Stage 1:** holiday topic; **Writing Book:** copymasters 71, 72, 74.

# OUR TOWN

## ENGLISH

- Share views on 'good' and 'bad' features
- Read guides and information leaflets
- Write a tourist guide
- Compose town stories
- Write about the town in the future
- Write labels for displays

## HISTORY

- Investigate the origins of the settlement
- Study historic sources
- Make a town time line
- Study differences between past and present
- Visit a museum or site of historic interest
- Make a classroom museum of local history

## ART

- Sketch from field observations
- Representations of feelings about the town
- Model town buildings
- Discuss and portray town 'colours'
- Study work of local artists

## ENVIRONMENTAL EDUCATION AND CITIZENSHIP

- Follow a town trail
- Consider environmental enhancement
- Improve the school grounds

## OUR TOWN

## GEOGRAPHY

- Make maps and plans of the town
- Study local maps of various scales and types
- Look at aerial photographs
- Follow directions and routes
- Use geographical vocabulary
- Learn local names
- Study land use and features
- Contrast the town with others
- Investigate local industries
- Study buildings and their use
- Interview people who work in town
- Consider the size of the town
- Find out about goods, services and transportation
- Consider the purpose of the town
- Consider good and bad features
- Consider environmental changes

## DESIGN AND TECHNOLOGY

- Construct and use databases

## SCIENCE

- Make observations on town trails
- Study the town at different times
- Observe and record changes to natural life
- Explore a range of habitats
- Study building materials and the weathering process

## ECONOMIC AND INDUSTRIAL UNDERSTANDING

- Investigate local businesses and industries
- Interview a business person or industrialist

**IDEAS BANK**
General starting points: Suggestions for programmes of study of core and foundation subjects relating to topic, and links with cross-curricular themes and R.E.

**STARTING POINTS**
● Make a collection of maps and photographs (including aerial photographs) of your town, as it exists at the present time and in days gone by.

● Undertake a discussion of children's key thoughts about their town – what they like best about it, what they think could be improved, favourite landmarks, etc.
● Go out and explore the town through fieldwork: a local neighbourhood walk, visit to a shopping centre, railway station, museum, etc.

# HISTORY

**Areas of study (Key Elements 1-5)**
● Look at a series of photographs, news reports and other historic sources about the town or your local neighbourhood. Place these in sequence to show aspects of change and development through time. [1a-b]
● Focus on key landmarks or events shown in resources as described above and identify differences between past and present times, and between times in the past. [1a, 1b]
● Construct an illustrated time line on the classroom wall to show key events in the history and development of your town. [1a, 1b]
● Let the children work in pairs or groups, each with a historical photograph, map or news item about the town. Share ideas about what can be learned from the resource. [1a-b]
● Visit a museum or local studies department of your library: study a range of sources which help the children

to identify with and to find out about their town's past. [1a-b, 2, 3]
● If possible, arrange to borrow relevant photographs and copies of maps for classroom interpretation. These are often available through a museum or library educational loan service. [1a-b]
● Augment the above, or start your own 'museum of local history' in the classroom, with reference material provided by yourself and the children's families – perhaps relatives may have photographs and artefacts from the local area that have passed through generations. [1a-b]
● Visit a particular historical site in town, perhaps the oldest building, a historic house, the site of a Roman camp or a National Trust property. Discuss how such a place can help us to find out about how people lived long ago, and to answer other questions about the past. [1a-b, 2, 3]

# GEOGRAPHY

**Geographical skills**
● Draw maps of your local area, or certain routes of the town, if of appropriate size. Depending on the age and ability of the children, these maps may range from the spontaneous/pictorial to those with greater levels of detail and accuracy. [1a-c, 2, 3a, 3b, 3c, 3d, 3f]
● Study maps of various scales (such as Ordnance Survey maps, A-Z street maps, town visitors' guides) which show a range of information about the locality, and help the children to interpret them. [1a, 1b, 2, 3a, 3b, 3c, 3e]
● Look at aerial photographs of your neighbourhood, or of the whole town if it is of appropriate size. Identify features. Compare these with pictures of the area taken on the ground. [1a, 1b, 2, 3a, 3c, 3f]
● Go out into the town or neighbourhood: follow simple directions and routes using plans or simple maps. [1a, 1b, 2, 3a, 3b, 3c]
● Use geographical vocabulary (such as hill, slope, river, shopping district) to talk about places seen on visits out of the classroom. [1a, 1b, 2, 3a]

**Places and thematic study**
● Discuss with the children the name of where they live – their own street as well as the district or town name. Name familiar features of the local area, such as the name of the railway station, a nearby river, shopping centre, housing estate, and so on. [4, 5a]
● Let the children write out their full addresses, including the name of the town, county and country where they live. [4]
● Describe the uses of land and buildings in your locality/town. [5b, 5d]
● Compare and contrast your home town with another locality. [4, 5a, 5b, 5c, 5d, 6a, 6b]
● Discuss industries/activities in the town and help children appreciate why they are located where they are. [4, 5a, 5b, 5c, 5d]
● Go out and investigate a familiar landscape feature in the town (for example, a river, hill, canal, etc.) Help the children to identify and describe this feature. [5a]
● Study a range of buildings in the town, to demonstrate that these are used for different purposes. [5d]

- Invite one or more visitors (for example, police officer, bank manager, railway employee, shopkeeper) to talk to the children about their work in the local area. Help the children to pre-structure the interview, so that they find out about how these people relate to the community, its buildings, where they live, etc. [5c, 5d]
- Discuss the size of your town compared to other familiar places. [4,6b]
- Find out what goods and services are needed by the town community (which will clearly vary depending on the size and location of the settlement) and how they are provided. [4,5b,5d]
- Study all forms of transport used in the town – perhaps car, rail, bus, air, underground – and discuss why, when and by whom these different forms are used. [6b, 6c]

- Explore the town to find any features which reveal its function or origins. [4, 5a, 5b, 5c, 5d]
- Discuss whether the town has a specific prime purpose, for example, a residential area, the site of a particular industry, etc. [4,5a,5d]
- Ask the children's views on the best features of their settlement. Are there places, areas or features within it which they do not like? [6a]
- Go on a town walk or trail to spot ways in which people have changed features or aspects of the environment. [6b]
- Write about and illustrate with 'before and after' pictures, actions or activities that have been designed to improve the town. Let the children express their views about whether these attempts have been successful. [6c]

# ENGLISH ▶

### Speaking and listening
- Let the children talk and share views on 'good' and 'bad' features of their town, discussing how aspects could be improved, why they like particular locations and features, and the success of attempts to improve aspects of its environment. [1a-1d, 2a, 2b, 3a, 3b]

### Reading
- Collect tourist guides, information leaflets and news cuttings relating to the town. These can be used to support many activities in history and geography. With younger children, appropriate sentences based on such information sources could be written out on to cards for the children to read aloud. [1b, 1c, 2a, 2b, 2d]

### Writing
- Provide a series of words or short sentences about your town. Ask the children to expand on these and organise them into a piece of writing that would help visitors to learn about the place. [1a, 1b, 1c, 2a, 2b, 2c, 2d, 3a, 3b]
- Write a tourist guide for your town. Children could work individually or in groups on various sections of such a guide. [1a, 1b, 1c, 2a, 2b, 2c, 2d, 3a, 3b]
- Let the children compose imaginary stories set in particular buildings, streets or locations known to the class. [1a, 1b, 1c, 2a, 2b, 2c, 2d, 3a, 3b]
- Write stories entitled 'Our Town: 21st Century', giving views on how the town may change in the future. [1a, 1b, 1c, 2a, 2b, 2c, 2d, 3a, 3b]
- Prepare labels for wall displays, models and other art and craft work related to the project. These can be of varying complexity depending on the age of the children. [1a, 1b, 1c, 2a, 2b, 2c, 2d, 3a, 3b]

# SCIENCE ▶

All the activities marked with an asterisk below provide opportunities for experimental and investigative science.

### Experimental and investigative science
- *Go out on town trails to complete a series of planned observations, for example, of building materials, urban wildlife, wild flowers, garden flowers, trees, birds, etc. Select and use appropriate recording techniques [1a, 1b, 1c, 2a, 2b, 2c, 3a, 3b, 3c, 3d, 3e, 3f]
- *Observe aspects of the built and natural environments in different seasons, weather conditions or at different times of the day. Pursue both spontaneous and planned observations – i.e. those designed to test a particular idea or hypothesis, for example, that a town street may have more animal and bird visitors at a certain time of day. [1a, 1b, 1c, 2a, 2b, 2c, 3a, 3b, 3c, 3d, 3e, 3f]

### Life processes and living things
- *If possible, find a part of town where human activity is changing the environment – for example, a building plot, site of demolition, change of land use. Design investigations to observe and record how such changes are affecting plant and animal life. [5a, 5b]
- Explore different habitats in town and their range of plant and animal life, helping children to appreciate that different kinds of living things have their own 'niches' and are found in different localities – for example, walls, gardens, wasteland, roadsides, trees, ponds, and so on. [1b, 4b, 5a, 5b]

### Materials and their properties
- *Observe and record a range of building materials (for walls, roofs, doors, fences, etc.) in particular streets

or in the town as a whole. Detailed studies could be done of specific buildings as well as broad surveys. See whether particular materials are dominant. Compare and contrast with materials used in other towns, if field visits are possible. [1a, 1b, 1c, 1d, 1e]

● Discuss which building materials occur naturally and which are made from raw materials. [1a, 1b, 1c, 1d, 1e, 2a, 2b]
● Look for and discuss changes that have occurred to buildings as a result of weathering. [2a, 2b]

# TECHNOLOGY

**Information technology**
● Use data collected on field visits (for example, on wildlife, traffic counts, building use and materials) and enter into databases. Select and retrieve information as and when appropriate to link with other tasks. [1a, 1b, 1c, 2a, 2b, 2c]

# ART

**Investigating and making**
● Make sketches, paintings or collages to record observations from direct experience in the town.
● Make collages and paintings which represent the children's ideas of their favourite and least favourite parts of town – responding both to memory and imagination.
● Construct models of selected town buildings, or of the whole settlement if of appropriate size.
● Discuss and portray through a variety of media the 'colours' of your town – perhaps there are 'grey' (industrial) zones, 'green' parklands and 'colourful' shopping precincts.

**Knowledge and understanding**
● Visit the local art gallery and find any recognised works of art based upon the local area that have been displayed. Look at and discuss these – what can they tell us about the town now or in the past?

# ENVIRONMENTAL EDUCATION AND CITIZENSHIP

**Environmental education and citizenship**
● Follow a town trail: take the children on a walk which takes in a variety of town locations (residential streets, shopping area, park, etc.). Observe ways in which people can enhance and also spoil the world around them. Use this as the basis for a discussion on the need to take care of our world and ways in which we can do this.
● Following on from the above, discuss and plan a project which involves the class in enhancing their town in some way – perhaps by picking up litter, planting trees or flowers, or establishing bird boxes.
● Engage the class in activities which enhance and improve the quality of the school grounds and buildings. Help pupils to appreciate that the local environment of the school contributes to the overall quality of neighbourhood appearance.

# ECONOMIC AND INDUSTRIAL UNDERSTANDING

● Find out the names of some significant local businesses or industries. Discuss whether a range of these exists in the town, or whether the area is noted for one particular economic activity. If appropriate, discuss why this is so – perhaps local availability of certain resources.

● Invite a representative of a significant town business or industrial activity to come and talk to the children in simple terms about why the activity is located where it is, who/how many people are employed, what they do, and who it serves.

**Blueprints links**
**Art Key Stage 1:** activities 39, 45; **Art Resource Bank:** copymaster 92; **Geography Key Stage 1:** many activities and copymasters including sections on local fieldwork, the school locality, houses, shops and services and journeys; **History Key Stage 1:** copymasters 65, 55, 67, 69, 82, 83, 85–89; **Infant Geography Resource Bank:** section on homes and settlements and different places, copymasters 1–25, 69–81; **Religious Education Key Stage 1:** copymasters 41–42; **Second Key Stage 1 Topics Book:** complete topic on where we live with copymasters; **Writing Book:** copymaster 48.

# UNDERGROUND

## ENGLISH

- Name things from underground
- Visit somewhere underground
- Read poems and stories about being underground
- Talk about safety underground
- Describe places underground
- Read and research about underground
- Make a 'World Underground' book
- Write stories about underground

## MUSIC

- Make echoes and compose underground music
- Listen to 'underground' music

## ENVIRONMENTAL EDUCATION

- Discuss conservation of the Earth's surface

## ART

- Make cave paintings
- Make rubbings of hole covers
- Use clay
- Make an underground frieze
- Make cave pictures

## DESIGN AND TECHNOLOGY

- Identify needs for lifting gear
- Design, plan, make and evaluate lifting gear

## UNDERGROUND

## GEOGRAPHY

- Look for 'holes' leading underground
- Observe falling rainwater
- Learn about underground water
- Find out about weathering
- Visit caves
- Find out about landscape features
- Investigate underground transport
- Study coal mining
- Investigate other underground resource
- Find out about impacts of extracting resources

## HISTORY

- Learn about the history of mining
- Find out about origins of underground transport
- Research cave paintings

## P.E.

- Perform 'underground' movements

## R.E.

- Talk about burial customs
- Visit a graveyard
- Tell the Resurrection story

## SCIENCE

- Dig into the ground
- Collect soil samples and study soil
- Set up a wormery
- Investigate plants' needs in the ground
- Name underground plant parts
- Observe and study roots
- Study invertebrates
- Keep an underground creature
- Observe decomposition
- Set up a compost heap
- Study fuels from below ground

**IDEAS BANK**
General starting points: Suggestions for programmes of study of core and foundation subjects relating to topic, and links with cross-curricular themes and R.E.

**STARTING POINTS**
● Observe or keep in the classroom creature(s) which live or burrow underground, such as worms or gerbils.
● Make a collection of things which go, live or come from underground – for example, some forms of transport, drainage pipes, some animals, roots, coal, caves, etc.
● Make a visit underground – perhaps travel on a form of underground transport, visit a cave or cellar.
● Contact organisations which deal with underground subjects, such as the Coal Board or London Transport, and collect materials for display and discussion.

# ENGLISH ▶

**Speaking and listening**
● Go around the class asking each child to name something which goes, lives or comes from under the ground. [1a, 1b, 1c, 2a-b, 3a-b]
● After a visit underground (on transport, cellar to a mining museum or cave, etc.) discuss what it feels like to be below the surface of the ground – and differences between being above and below ground level. [1a, 1b, 1c, 1d, 2a-b, 3a-b]
● Read (for the children to listen and respond to) a number of poems and stories about life underground, such as 'Journey To The Centre Of The Earth' by Jules Verne, Tolkien's 'The Hobbit', Ivan Southall's 'The Fox Hole', 'Watership Down' by Richard Adams, the Greek legend of Theseus and the Minotaur, or real-life tales about Lord Shaftesbury and the plight of children working in the coal mines during the nineteenth century. [1a, 1b, 1c, 2a-b, 3a-b]
● If you are going on an underground visit of any kind, have the children listen very carefully to instructions regarding behaviour and safety, and discuss why related rules are necessary. [1c]

**Reading**
● Write out a set of simple word cards describing places underground. Ask the children to match these to a set of pictures (for example, of a cellar, mine, tunnel, cave, hole, burrow, station, etc.) [1b, 1c, 2a, 2b]

● Provide reading material for the children to read and research from themselves – stories, reference books, poems and other writing on underground themes – and engage in discussion on material you have read out loud. [1a-d, 2a-d, 3]

**Writing**
● Compile a class book of 'The World Underground'. Divide children into pairs or small groups, each to research, write stories and factual accounts about and illustrate a different aspect of underground life – for example, transport underground, animals underground, minibeasts underground, coal mining (both nowadays and in the nineteenth century, when young children were compelled to spend many hours a day working underground), precious stones and metals, underground tunnels, cellars, underground services such as gas, water and sewage, fossils in the ground, and so on. [1a-c, 2a-c, 3a-b]
● Write imaginary stories with titles such as 'Underground Adventure', 'Lost Underground', 'The Strange Creature Who Never Surfaces', 'Who Is In The Hole?', 'Underground Treasure', 'Underground Monster', 'The Escape Tunnel', and so on. [1a-c, 2a-c, 3a-b]
● Write stories about real-life situations that may happen underground – for example, 'The Lost Rabbit', 'Exploring The Cave', 'Mining Discovery', 'Digging The Channel Tunnel', 'Strike On The Underground', etc. [1a-c, 2a-c, 3a-b]

# SCIENCE ▶

**Experimental and investigative science**
● All activities below provide opportunities for experimental and investigative science.
● Go out into the school grounds, a garden or suitable wasteland area. Dig into the ground and observe what is revealed – perhaps stones, leaves, twigs, worms, insects. [1a-c, 2a-c, 3a-f]
● Repeat the above activity in a series of locations and over a period of time, noting changes and differences between sites. [1a-c, 2a-c, 3a-f]
● Collect soil samples from various locations. Take them back to the classroom and observe under a microscope. Pursue a sub-topic on soil and its formation. [1a-c, 2a-c, 3a-f]
● Set up a wormery in the classroom, and use this for observation, investigations and testing of various hypotheses, for example, what would happen if leaves of various types were placed on the surface. Help children to appreciate the need for a fair test. [1a-c, 2a-c, 3a-f]
● Devise investigations to include regular observations, predictions and measuring, which focus on germinating and growing plants with and without their roots in soil. (Relate to Life processes and living things). [1a-c, 2a-c, 3a-f]

## Life processes and living things

- Find out the names of parts of plants which live under the ground; investigate various types of root, bulbs and tubers. [3a-c, 4b, 5a-b]
- Observe the roots of various plants: study the ground beneath a mature tree; carefully remove a pot plant from its container to reveal the root ball and then replace it; grow bulbs and broad bean seeds in water, and watch the roots grow. Find out the importance of root systems. [3a-c, 4b, 5a-b]
- By careful digging and removal of leaf litter, collect some invertebrates from under the ground. Keep in a carefully planned tank of moist soil in the classroom for a day or two for observations, identification and investigations. [1a, 3a-c, 4a-b]
- Keep an animal (in carefully researched and planned conditions) in the classroom which burrows or tunnels into the ground: for example, set up a gerbil tank. Observe it regularly, and learn conditions necessary to keep the creature(s) alive and well. [1a-b, 4b, 5a-b]
- Find woodland or wasteland areas where you can dig below the surface without harming plants. Make digs to observe leaf litter and evidence of decaying materials below the surface. Relate to the role of bacteria and invertebrates in the soil. [1a, 5a-b]
- Follow on from the above by setting up a compost heap. Observe decay over a period of time. [1a]

## Materials and their properties

- Consult leaflets and reference books to find out about fuels used in the home, and which have links with the world underground. Make a display of pictures of fuels which have such links, such as coal from mines, gas which comes from below ground and travels along underground pipes, oil from wells, etc. [1a-e]

# GEOGRAPHY ▶

## Geographical skills and places

- Go out into your neighbourhood and hunt for 'holes' which lead underground (entrances to underground stations, manhole covers, drains, holes made in the road by workmen, entrances to animal homes, holes dug by builders for foundations, tunnels for trains and canals, etc.) Find out more about these and perhaps record them on a map of your area. [1a, 1b, 2, 3a-f, 4, 5a, 5d]
- Observe rainwater falling on the ground – both on roadways and countryside. Find out where it goes to (leading to further research on drains, sewers, and seeping of water into the ground.) [1a-c, 2, 3a-f, 4, 5a, 5c, 5d]
- Consult reference books to find out more about underground water: underground streams, the soaking of rainwater down to underground rocks, and its weathering effects. [1a-c, 2, 3a, 3e, 3f, 4, 5a, 5c]
- Pursue the above to find out more about the effects of weathering on the formation of underground passages and caves. If possible, visit some caves. [1a-c, 2, 3a, 3e, 3f, 4, 5a, 5c]
- Find out about other landscape features which exist in part underground, for example, volcanoes and geysers. [1c, 2, 3e, 3f]
- Conduct a sub-topic on underground transport – perhaps focusing on the London underground system, or that of a city nearer to your own home; find out about the building of the Channel Tunnel, and other tunnels used to transport people and goods beneath the ground. [1a-c, 2, 3f, 4, 5a, 5b, 5d]
- Find out about coal mining – where coal is mined, the procedures used and 'a day in the life of a mine-worker'. [1c, 2, 3e, 3f, 4, 5a, 5b, 5d]
- Find out about other resources obtained from beneath the Earth's surface – for example, oil, minerals, precious metals and stones. [1c, 2, 3e, 3f, 4, 5a, 5b, 5d]

## Geographical skills and thematic study

- Discuss how extracting resources from beneath the ground affects the surface environment. [1a-c, 2, 3f, 4, 5a, 5b, 5d, 6a-c]

# HISTORY ▶

## Areas of study (Key Elements 1-5)

- Use reference books, and perhaps visit a museum or mining heritage site to find out about how the coal mining industry has changed through time. Write accounts about 'mining past and present', and 'a day in the life of an early miner'. [1a-b, 2]
- Extend this activity to include research work on 'forty-niners' and the gold rush in California and/or the diamond mines of South Africa. [1b, 3]
- Find out when and where the first UK underground transport system opened, and how it operated. Compare this with modern systems. [1a-b]
- Research the origins of cave paintings such as those at Lascaux in France, and find out more about the lives of early people. [1b, 2]

# DESIGN AND TECHNOLOGY

**Design and technology capability**
*Discuss how certain things found underground need to be raised to the surface. Identify the need for lifting gear. [1a-c, 2a-c]

**Designing skills**
● Design lifting gear to meet a specific purpose in the classroom. [3a-f]

**Making skills and knowledge and understanding**
● Considering constraints and materials available, plan and make lifting gear which responds to your identified needs. [4a-f]
● Describe the results of your lifting gear design, and see if the device works over a sustained period of time. [4f]

# ART

**Investigating and making**
● Make cave paintings. Paint the outline of large caves on the classroom wall and let the children paint images in the tradition of ancient history.
● Make rubbings of manhole covers, hydrant covers and any other entrances to the underground world that you can find.
● Talk about clay as a medium which originates under the ground. Use clay for making pots and ornaments.
● Make a large wall frieze of 'life under the earth's surface'. Print a soil effect using brown paint on foam or polystyrene blocks. Leave spaces for small tunnels. Add collage or painted pictures of creatures which may inhabit your underground world, and annotate with words to label your creatures and their homes (crevice, warren, burrow, earth, sett, etc.).
● The subject of caves has exciting scope for art and craft work. Talk about colours and choose appropriate materials to make pictures and collages of damp caves with stalactites and stalagmites.
● Mythology tells tales of dragons guarding hoards of gold and jewels in underground lairs – another source of colourful art and craft work, in terms of paintings and/or models of these creatures and their treasures.

# MUSIC

**Performing and composing**
● Make echoes like those you might hear in underground caves. Try this in rooms, bottles and boxes. Use your echoes together with 'spooky' underground sounds made on instruments to compose your own 'Music of the Underground'. Perform and record it.

**Listening and appraising**
● Listen to any well-known music you can find with an underground theme, such as 'Fingal's Cave' (The Hebrides Overture) by Mendelssohn, extracts from 'Peer Gynt' by Grieg, and at a more contemporary level the Rick Wakeman concept album of rock music, 'Journey To The Centre Of The Earth' (LP Number AMLH 63621, CD Number Spectrum Music 550 06120) which was inspired by the Jules Verne novel.
● Let the children hear some of the folk songs associated with the early days of coal mining ('The Big Hewer', 'Down In The Coal Mine' or 'The Gresford Disaster', recorded by artists such as Ewan McColl or the Ian Campbell Folk Group) which describe the triumphs and tragedies of this bygone working life.

# P.E.

● Perform movements associated with various forms of work and activity underground, such as pulling, digging, heaving up, burrowing, climbing up, wriggling along, climbing down, and so on.

# ENVIRONMENTAL EDUCATION ▶

- Talk about the fact that the earth's surface is a very important part of our world. Discuss how certain actions such as removing plants from the ground, mining or quarrying can harm the Earth in various ways.

- Talk about the custom of burial in the ground which has been practised for centuries by many cultures and religions.

# R.E. ▶

- Visit a graveyard. With the vicar's permission, and with suitable attention to behaviour, study the gravestones and see what you can learn about people in the past.

  Of course, these two activities should be conducted with sensitivity, particularly if any child has suffered a recent bereavement in his/her family.

- Tell the story of the resurrection of Jesus Christ, and the Christian belief that he came back from the dead after being buried in a tomb in the grounds of the Garden of Gethsemane.

**Blueprints links**
**Festivals:** page 78 (colliery festivals); **History Key Stage 1:** copymaster 88 (children down mines); **Environmental Education Key Stage 1:** copymaster 39 (decomposition); **Geography Key Stage 1:** copymaster 45 (quarry); **Health Education Key Stage 1:** copymaster 94 (coal-mines); **Infant Geography Resource Bank:** copymasters 61–65 (mining coal and clay); **Science Key Stage 1:** copymaster 27 (decomposition); **Seasonal Topics:** Autumn copymaster 8 (fungi); **Topics 5–8:** complete topic on underground with copymasters.

# PETS

## ENGLISH

- Discuss new pet introduced into classroom and select a name for it
- Study pet equipment and talk about pets in general
- Make a list of pets and sort them into groups
- Define the meaning of 'pet'
- Write and talk about individual pets
- Listen to stories and poems relating to pets. Discuss these
- Write imaginary stories about pets
- Use reference books to acquire information
- Make topic books
- Factual writing about any school visits; pets, their origins, health, habits, etc.
- Keep a diary about classroom pet

## SCIENCE

- Learn about basic life processes of living creatures
- Study different groups of animals, with special reference to pets
- Look at wild and tame creatures and talk about these in relation to pets

## HEALTH EDUCATION

- Talk about the importance of cleanliness
- Discuss danger from other people's animals

## MATHEMATICS

- Construct diagrams, charts, graphs, etc. relevant to topic
- Sort pictures of pets (or animals in general) into groups
- Construct simple data-base

## ART

- Make range of 'pet' pictures
- Design and make a wall frieze
- Make two-dimensional pet pictures using geometric shapes
- Use clay to model pets
- Make pet puppets
- Make soft toys
- Create fantasy pets
- Study and discuss art-work relating to pets including historical paintings

## DESIGN AND TECHNOLOGY

- Plan to design an attractive pet enclosure
- Design, plan, make and evaluate model pet 'houses'

## INFORMATION TECHNOLOGY

- Prepare simple database

## HISTORY

- Look at 'pet' pictures from the past
- Talk about attitudes towards pets
- Discuss Egyptian cats as 'gods'
- Read/tell true/fictional stories about pets
- Make deductions from historical pictures/artefacts

## R.E.

- Talk about the Creation
- Discuss treatment of 'pet' animals both in the past and today, including relevant laws in this country
- Talk about work of charities such as Guide Dogs for the Blind

**IDEAS BANK**
General starting points: Suggestions for programmes of study of core and foundation subjects relating to topic, and links with cross-curricular themes and R.E.

**STARTING POINTS**
● Introduce a pet into the classroom, but first ensure that it can be secure and adequately cared for during weekends, holidays, cold nights and so on.
● Arrange a small display of pet equipment, for example, a dog lead, a feeding bowl, a bird's perch, a cat's toy, and so on.

● If possible, arrange a visit from a representative of a local animal/bird sanctuary, preferably someone who will bring animals/birds with them and talk to the children about them.
● Arrange a visit from a 'Guide Dogs for the Blind' representative.
● Organise a display of books, pictures and so on relating to pets. Ask the children to bring in books, pictures, etc. of their own, to contribute to a class display.
● Tell or read stories and poems about pets.

# ENGLISH ▶

**Speaking and listening**
● As a class study the new pet which is being introduced into the classroom. Talk about its species and what must be done to keep it healthy and contented. Let the children suggest names for their pet and vote for the most popular name. [1a-c, 2a-b]
● Look at various equipment designed for pets and let the children link each item with a popular pet. This can be done as a drawing/writing exercise if desired. [1c]
● Tell the children to write the names of (or draw) as many pets as they can. Compile a class list and, after discussion with the children, sort the pets into specified groups. When discussing how to group the pets, talk about strange/unusual pets kept by some people, for example snakes, tarantula spiders and so on. Also discuss 'working' pets such as guide dogs, some horses, police dogs, etc. [1a-c]
● Ask the children to write down or say their definitions of the word 'pet'. What meanings does the word convey? Discuss the various ideas and establish a general concensus about the meaning of the word. (1a-c, 2a)
● Let the children talk about their own pets and others of which they have knowledge. [1a-c, 2a-b]
● Tell or read some stories/poems about pets. Talk about them all with the class and encourage individual contributions. [1a-c, 2a-b]
● Let the children work in pairs or small groups, to plan an imaginary story about a pet of their choice. When they are ready, let them tell their stories, or act them, to the rest of the class. [1a-c, 2a-b]

**Reading**
● Discuss the contents of stories and poems when they are told or read to the children. Give them the opportunity to read a poem or part of a story aloud to the class; this could be a chosen passage/poem from a book brought into school by the child. [1a, c-d]
● Begin a story about a chosen pet, perhaps with a title like 'The Day Sid Escaped' or 'When I Found Peta'. Ask the children to continue the story and complete it. Let them read or tell their stories to the rest of the class. (1a, c-d, 2c)
● Include reference/factual books in any class display about pets and encourage the children to use these. Show them how to look for information when it is printed in alphabetical order. [1b, 2d]

**Writing**
● Write and illustrate imaginative stories/poems about pets, for example, 'My Pet Saved My Life', 'My Secret Pet', 'When I Lost Tabby', 'The Day Digger was Stolen', etc. [1a-c, 2a-b]
● Make a class, or individual, 'Pet' book to include all writing, drawing, graphs, charts, etc. [1a-c, 2a-b]
● Write informative labels about pictures and other work on display. [1a-c, 2a-b]
● Write factual accounts of any school visits or about visitors and their pets in school. [1a-c, 2a-b]
● Keep a diary, or write about the classroom pet, its habits, growth, what happens at weekends/holidays, who cares for it, and so on. [1a-c, 2a-b]
● Write factually about animals in general (Science), and pets of the past (History). [1a-c, 2a-b]

# SCIENCE ▶

**Experimental and investigative science**
● Encourage the children to observe closely the living habits of their school pet, to discuss these and compare with like creatures at home or in the wild. [2a-c, 3a, 3c-d]

**Life processess and living things**
● Talk and write about living things in general and

relate to the lives of particular pets. Discuss the basic life processes common to both humans and other animals. Include reproduction, if appropriate, movement, the senses, etc. [1a-b]
● Discuss classification of animals and help the children to group them into broad groups, for example those found on/in water, air and land. Other groups can then be chosen, say, animals which live under-

ground/on the surface, night/day creatures, and so on. Point out some observable differences. Make special reference to particular pets and the groups which they may be included in. [4b, 5a]
● Investigate some of the differences between pet animals and those in the wild. Look at features which

are relevant to both, for example food, safety and so on. Ask the children to write down their findings. Discuss those pets whose natural homes are in other countries, perhaps with a different climate. How have they adapted to the British climate? [4b, 5a]

# MATHEMATICS

### Using and applying mathematics
Activities below provide opportunities for using and applying mathematics.
● Let the children select the appropriate materials and mathematics for recording statistics relevant to their 'pets' topic. [1a, 2a-d, 3c-d, 4a]

### Number
● Let children sort pictures of pets and describe the criteria chosen for grouping them. [5a]

● Help the children to plan graphs and/or other diagrams relating to the topic, showing, for example, the most popular pet in the class/school, the most popular colour of budgerigar, the three most popular pet names, etc. [5b]
● Construct a simple database for each child, based on, for example, pets they own, pets they know, favourite pet, least favourite pet, etc. Let the children have practice with the computer in learning how to access and retrieve information. [5b]

# DESIGN AND TECHNOLOGY

### Designing skills
● Talk with the children about the needs of pets, for example, space to move, food, warmth and so on. Relate this to an animal's pen, cage, aquarium, hutch, etc. Suggest that while most enclosures are adequate, they may not be visually attractive. See if the children can design and make a model pen or cage which would be both suitable for an animal and pleasing to look at. [3a-b]
● Let the children work in small groups to discuss and plan a suitable enclosure for a specified animal. Ask them to draw their ideas, and proposed plans on paper,

making relevant notes. Discuss these with the groups. [3a-f]

### Making skills and knowledge and understanding
● Working in their groups let the children select appropriate materials from as wide a range as possible and, with discussion and help where required, let them make their chosen enclosure. [4a-e]
● Let each group show its completed model to the rest of the class. Encourage all the children to discuss their efforts, the problems encountered and whether they are satisfied with the finished product. [4f]

# INFORMATION TECHNOLOGY

### Information technology
● Prepare a simple database to show details of specified groups of animals, individual choice of pets, and so

on. Help the children to enter data into the computer, and to amend and retrieve information when necessary. [1a, 2a-c]

# ART

### Investigating and making
● Using a wide range of materials, let the children create a variety of 'pet' pictures. Make a wall display of these.
● Help the children to design a wall frieze with a 'pet' theme, this could be as simple as 'Mary Had a Little Lamb' or more complex showing a variety of pets or pets

through history for example. Ensure all the children contribute to this.
● Make 'pet' mobiles.
● Use two-dimensional shapes to make 'pet' pictures.
● Use clay to model three-dimensional pets. Let the children research pictures to help with the making of these.

- Make 'pet' puppets.
- Let the children make soft toys depicting their favourite pets.
- Introduce a fantasy element into the artwork by letting the children create imaginary pets, e.g. space pets, 'lost-world' pets, etc.

**Knowledge and understanding**
- Try to show the children a variety of artwork relating to 'pets' including prints of historical paintings, pictures on vases, urns, postcards and so on. Discuss these and the different techniques used to depict the animals.

# HISTORY

**Range and depth of historical knowledge and understanding**
- Show the children some historical pictures of pets, for example Victorian birds in ornate bird cages, Egyptian cats, and so on. Discuss differing attitudes towards pets, for example cats treated as gods in Egyptian times or the Victorian fashion to cage exotic song-birds. Talk about dancing bears, performing monkeys and so on. Would the children class these as pets? Which animals have been pets, as we know them, for hundreds of years? Read or tell some stories about pets in the past. [2a-c]

**Interpretations of history**
- Tell or read some true stories about pets, as well as fictional ones. Discuss the difference between the two and how stories can change in the telling. Talk about fact and point of view and relate this to real stories from either the present or history, for example 'The Faithful Dog' from '101 Assembly Stories' by Frank Carr, published by W Foulsham & Co Ltd. [3a]

**Historical enquiry**
- Look at historical pictures or artefacts relating to pets and let the children talk about what can be learned from them. [4a-b]

# R.E.

- Discuss the Creation and God's love for all living things. Talk to the children about our responsibilities in relation to animals and the application of these especially when we have a pet or pets of our own.
- Talk about the past when people could cage any wild animal or bird and how laws have been passed to try to eliminate this cruelty to wild animals. Make sure the children know the difference between pets bred in captivity over many years and wild animals who are used to being free. Stress the responsibility for care and love

when one owns a pet.
- Discuss the work of the RSPCA, the PDSA and similar organisations.
- Talk about the animals which are pets but also work for us, such as guide dogs.
- This might be an opportunity to plan a fund-raising event, to raise money for a chosen animal charity.
- Tell the children the story of St. Francis of Assisi and the legends linked with his name.

# HEALTH EDUCATION

**Health education**
- Stress the importance of keeping all pets well fed, healthy and clean. Remind the children that it is very important for them to keep healthy and clean also, and as it is possible for pets to carry some harmful germs, they must always wash their hands after cleaning out pens etc.

- It might also be a good opportunity to reinforce the possible danger of approaching strange dogs or getting any dog too excited. Explain to the children that animals do not think like we do and biting is a natural part of their playing/fighting.

**Blueprints links**
**Art Key Stage 1:** complete topic on living things, many copymasters; **Art Resource Bank:** complete chapters on animals and birds, copymasters 1–27, 90; **Early Years Songs and Rhymes:** many songs and rhymes on the topic; **Health Education Key Stage 1:** copymaster 24; **History Key Stage 1:** topic and copymasters on people and animals; **Poetry Book:** section on animals, copymasters 1–4; **Religious Education Key Stage 1:** copymasters 7, 86; **Science Key Stage 1:** activities in Life processes and living things, and copymaster 21; **Topics 5–8:** complete topic on pets with copymasters; **Technology Key Stage 1:** many activities and copymasters: **Writing 5–8:** copymasters 2, 7, 13, 23, 35, 54; **Writing Book:** copymasters 29, 38, 49, 79.

# BIRTHDAYS

## ENGLISH

- Discuss the word 'birthday'
- Talk about birthdays
- Learn months of the year
- Write words about birthday memories
- Write stories about birthdays – past and future, real and imaginary
- Leap year birthdays

## MATHEMATICS

- Draw graphs and diagrams to represent birthday data
- Use a birthday database
- Do birthday number work
- Do a school birthday survey

## MUSIC

- Learn birthday songs
- Write your own birthday song and tune

## ART

- Design and make birthday cards
- Make a birthday cake
- Make zodiac pictures
- Make a Happy Birthday frieze
- Look at the work of artists in depicting Jesus' birth

## GEOGRAPHY

- Investigate birthday celebrations in distant lands

## BIRTHDAYS

## HISTORY

- Discuss your own birthday celebrations through time
- Find out about parents' and grandparents' birthdays
- Think of the children's past birthdays
- Interpreting birthday memories
- Write words about birthday memories
- Write stories about birthdays – past and future, real and imaginary

## R.E.

- Tell the story of Jesus' birth
- Research other famous birthdays
- Tell the Creation story and consider conflicting views

## SCIENCE

- Research how all things begin life
- Classify living things according to way of 'birth'
- Learn about human gestation
- Investigate animal gestation
- Observe the birth of animals
- Find out about twin births
- Consider the world's 'birthday'
- Consider yearly patterns
- Identify seasons of birth
- Investigate star signs
- Discuss horoscopes

**IDEAS BANK**
General starting points: Suggestions for programmes of study of core and foundation subjects relating to topic, and links with cross-curricular themes and R.E.

**STARTING POINTS**
● Make a birthday chart or diary: illustrate the birthdays of all the children in your class on a large plan of the year for display on the classroom wall.

● Commence the topic on a well-known birthday, for example, that of a famous person such as the Queen, or on your school's birthday.
● If your school is not accustomed to celebrating its birthday, find out when it was officially opened and begin a tradition by organising a birthday event on the appropriate day.
● Begin the topic on your own birthday, being prepared to share with the class ideas on how your birthday celebrations have changed over the years.

# HISTORY

**Areas of study (Key Elements 1-5)**
● Use your own birthday as an opportunity to discuss how objects and events have changed through time. Share ideas on how your celebrations and presents have changed over the years. For young teachers, this could be supplemented with stories of your parents' and grandparents' birthdays. [1a-b, 3]
● Augment the above activity by asking the children to talk to their parents and grandparents in order to have some sense of how birthday celebrations have changed over the years, and to develop a sense of chronology. [1a-b, 3]
● See if the children can recall their own birthdays of the past and anything special that happened on that day. Ask them to talk and write about these in sequence, if possible: for example, 'On my fourth birthday I ...', 'When I was five ...', 'On my sixth birthday ...' [1a-b, 3]

NOTE: The above, and all activities throughout the topic which involve children in discussion of personal birthdays should be treated with sensitivity, especially if there are children in the class who may not receive presents or have birthday celebrations.

● When discussing your own 'historic' birthdays, recall what was very special or perhaps not so happy about some of them. Tell the children why, and use concrete examples if possible, helping them to distinguish between a fact and what is just your own thoughts or point of view. [1a-b]
● Try to obtain objects relating to birthdays of times gone by: perhaps historic cards from antique dealers or from your own collections, or examples of presents from bygone birthdays. Use these to communicate information, and to raise and answer questions about the past. [1a-b, 3]
● Research the dates when some famous people were born (and see if any children share the same birthday). Use secondary resources to try to find out more about life at the time when your chosen celebrities were born. [1b, 2]

(NOTE: It may be possible to obtain facsimile newspapers which were published on dates when the children or their chosen celebrities were born, so that the children can read about notable news events of the day.) [1a, 2a, 3a]

# ENGLISH

**Speaking and listening**
● Discuss the significance of the word 'birthday'. In discussion, help the children to appreciate that all living creatures have birthdays, and that humans in many countries like to find special ways of remembering the day on which they were born. [1a-d, 2a-b, 3]
● If a child in your class has a birthday during the time the birthday topic is under consideration, make this fact a feature and ask him/her to talk about this special day. Let the other children listen, ask questions and comment on what has been said about the event. [1a-d, 2a-b, 3]
● Ask the children to say the month of the year in which they were born, and (if they can find out) the day of the week on which they were born, thus helping them to learn these key words. Talk about leap year birthdays [1a-d, 2a-b]

**Reading**
Make a collection of birthday cards with simple verses.

Let the children read these aloud and discuss which they like best, and why. [1b, 1c, 2a, 2b, 2d]
● Read stories/poems relating to birthdays and ask the children to bring in any relevant books from home. Let them read a favourite poem or part of a story to the other children. [1a, 1c, 1d, 2a]
● Discuss the content/structure etc. of some of the birthday stories told/read to the children. [1a, 1c, 1d, 2c, 3]

**Writing**
● Ask the children to draw or paint a picture of a birthday they can remember. Annotate this with a word or key words that best describe it. [1a-c, 2a-e, 3a-b]
● Let them write stories about a birthday – perhaps a current birthday or a special party or present they can remember. [1a-c, 2a-e, 3a-b]
● Write and illustrate imaginative stories entitled 'The most exciting birthday present', 'The birthday surprise' or 'What an amazing party!' [1a-c, 2a-e, 3a-b]

- Following on from English and history activities, encourage the children to imagine themselves in the future and write about 'My 21st birthday', 'My 50th birthday', 'My 80th birthday' and so on, trying to imagine how they may feel and act at various stages in their lives. [1a-c, 2a-e, 3a-b]
- Write stories about the interesting situation of being born on February 29th. [1a-c, 2a-e, 3a-b]

# GEOGRAPHY ▶

### Geographical skills and places

- Find out about how birthdays are celebrated in distant lands. This information is not easily accessible from reference works: if possible, make personal contacts and exchange letters with ideas about this topic. Use this information as a starting point for developing knowledge of people and their ways of life in a foreign land. [1c, 2, 3e, 3f, 4, 5a-d]

# MATHEMATICS ▶

### Using and applying mathematics

All activities provide opportunities for using and applying mathematics.

### Number

- Use birthdays as a subject for devising interesting calculations for the children to work out – for example, 'after 6 more birthdays I shall be ____ years old', 'I need to have another ____ birthdays before I shall be 10'. [1a, 1e, 2a, 2b, 3c, 3d, 4a, 5b]
- Calculate such questions as 'how many months until my next birthday?', 'how many days until my next birthday?', and so on. [1a, 1e, 2a, 2b, 3c, 3d, 4a, 5b]

- Undertake a birthday survey in your school. Count how many children in the school were born in each month. Find the most commonly shared birthday month, and the most commonly shared day of the week. [1a, 1c-f, 2a, 2b, 3c, 3d, 3e, 4a-d, 5b]
- Collect data on birthdays of the children in the class – days of the week and months of the year when they were born. Draw graphs and other statistical diagrams to represent the data collected. [1e, 5b]
- Enter the information you have collected about the children's birthdays on to a suitable database, for retrieval as and when required. [1f, 5b]

# SCIENCE ▶

### Experimental and investigative science

All activities marked with an asterisk below provide opportunities for experimental and investigative science.

### Life processes and living things

- * Discuss the fact that all living things are 'born' in some way, leading to research on differences between animal and plant life. [1a-b, 2a-f, 3a-c, 4a-b, 5a-b]
- * Pursue the above by helping to develop an understanding of classification in the animal kingdom: find out which creatures are born from within their mother in the same manner as humans (mammals), which hatch from eggs, etc. [1b, 4b]
- * Undertake an in-depth sub-topic on human gestation and the birth process. [1b, 2e]
- * Find out about the lengths of animal gestation periods (a farmer would be a useful source of information). [1b]
- * If possible, arrange to visit a farm at a time when animals such as ewes and cows are giving birth, so that the children can have the exciting experience of witnessing a birthday. [1b]

- *Find out more about the development of twins, i.e. why sometimes two (or more) living things can share the same time of birth. [1b, 2e,4a]

### Physical processes

- Consider the concept of 'The Birthday Of The World', helping children to begin to learn about differing views on how and when the world began. [2e]
- Following on from the above, discuss the fact that, just as our own lives have a yearly pattern, so does that of the Earth. We count the years (starting each new year on January 1st) and each year has an identical pattern of months. Relate this to work on the seasons. [2e, 3e]
- Find out how many children in the class (or do a school survey) were born in each of the 4 seasons (defining the dates according to the Equinoxes/ Solstices). Record this information on graphs/ diagrams/databases. [2e. 3e]
- Discuss and find out more about 'star signs', i.e. that every person has a birth sign related to astrological patterns. Help the children to find out their own star sign if they do not already know it. [2e, 3e]

- Consult star maps (and encourage children to look at a real starry sky, if possible) to identify well known constellations and signs of the zodiac. [2e, 3e]
- Talk to the children about horoscopes – letting them know that some people believe in telling fortunes 'through the stars', though many other people do not think there is any truth in these predictions. What is true is that when each of us was born, there were stars in certain positions in the sky as well as the Earth, Sun and Moon. [2e, 3e]

# R.E.

- Remind the children of the story of one of the most famous births of all time – that of Jesus Christ.
- Research the birth-dates and related stories of key figures from other world religions.

- Pursue thoughts on the 'world's birthday' by telling the story of the Creation. Relate this to science activities, and differences in beliefs and/or theories (i.e. creation v evolution).

# ART

### Investigating and making
- Design and make birthday cards – for family, friends, class members, a member of the school community or even the school itself.
- Bake a birthday cake if you are celebrating a particular day, or design and create a model cake, paying attention to colours and surface design.
- Make zodiac pictures – cut star shapes from silver foil. Arrange and glue on black or dark blue paper in the pattern of zodiac constellations.
- Make a large 'Happy Birthday' frieze to cover the whole of a classroom wall. Let each child have his/her own space to display a picture of themselves (perhaps as a baby), details of their birth (where, when, day of week, etc.) and how old they are. Decorate the remaining space with designs for birthday cards, paintings of cakes, candles, parties, balloons, etc.

### Knowledge and understanding
- Show the children pictures/reproductions of well-known works of art depicting the birthday of Jesus. Discuss the feeling and mood of these illustrations, and use them as a basis for discussing how people and events have changed through time. (Link with history activities.)

# MUSIC

### Performing and composing
- Learn to sing well known published birthday songs such as 'Happy Birthday To You', 'We Wish You Many Happy Returns Of The Day', and 'Comes A Birthday'.
- Work with the children to write words for your own new Birthday Song – and, if possible, compose a tune and perform it for the school. Perhaps you could write a song for the birthday of the school itself, which could then be sung every year at this time.

### Listening and appraising
- See if you can find recordings of songs or pieces of music which were popular at around the day or date on which some of the children in your class were born. A number of reference books should be available in your local library to assist these researches. Ask the children to listen to the music and comment on the various changes in style which may have taken place over the years. What was 'Top Of The Pops' when YOU were born?

### Blueprints links
**Christmas Key Stage 1:** book on Christmas; **Christmas Art and Craft:** present making activities; **Health Education Key Stage 1:** copymaster 11; **History Key Stage 1:** topic on celebrations including birthdays; **Poetry Book:** copymaster 11; **Religious Education Key Stage 1:** complete topic and copymasters on birth celebrations; **Writing 5–8:** copymaster 21.

# YESTERDAYS

## ENGLISH

- Discuss everyday changes
- Examine and discuss artefacts from the past and compare with today's equivalent
- Read and tell stories and poems about the past
- Write imaginative stories about the past
- Label artefacts in class museum and write briefly about selected exhibits
- Write factually about changes and the immediate past (social, political, etc.)

## HEALTH EDUCATION

- Discuss use of fuels and taking care
- Study hygiene in the past
- Talk about advances in medicine

## GEOGRAPHY

- Investigate maps of the local area
- Prepare and use route maps
- Observe local buildings and interesting features en route
- Draw sketch maps or plans
- Study past and present pictures of the local area
- Learn about aerial photographs
- Write your home address
- Learn the name of your home country
- Investigate changes in the local area
- Study any source of natural materials in the local area

## ART

- Make a range of relevant pictures
- Study shape and form of various artefacts
- Make a 'Yesterdays' wall frieze
- Learn about art work at the period being studied
- Look at relevant paintings and other works of art

## MATHEMATICS

- Make a 'Years' number line
- Represent data pictorially and on a database

## HISTORY

- Tell stories from the past
- Use a timeline to display artefacts
- Investigate artefacts on display
- Invite senior citizens to talk about the past and changes they have seen in their lifetime
- Study pictures from the past and make deductions
- Investigate changes in people's lives over a period of time
- Discuss facts and fiction

## P.E.

- Learn some traditional games

## MUSIC

- Learn songs from the selected period
- Compose theme music
- Investigate singing games
- Listen to selected pieces of music by well-known composers

## SCIENCE

- Investigate the importance of fuels
- Learn about materials, natural and human-made. Arrange a classroom display
- Find out the origins of specified fuels
- Study differences between homes of the past and today
- Learn about heating homes and the use of gas and electricity

**IDEAS BANK**
General starting points: Suggestions for ATs of core and foundation subjects relating to topic, and links with cross-curricular themes and R.E.

**STARTING POINTS**
(NOTE: The activities which follow relate to a definition of 'Yesterdays' which refers to past time going back over a period of 100 years. Readers may wish to reduce or extend this period depending upon individual circumstances.)
● Have a collection of pictures, books and artefacts in the classroom relating to the past. If possible, teachers should include possessions of their own which may have special memories or significance. Talk to children about life today and new trends that have recently arrived on the scene – for example, different styles of shoes, clothes, household gadgets and so on. Explain that things are always changing (can they give some examples from their own experience?) and that they are going to look at some of the changes in life-styles since their great great (etc.) grandparents were alive.
● Discuss the pictures and artefacts in your classroom display, and ask the children to help make a class museum by bringing in relevant items from home. Who can bring in the oldest exhibit? Talk about all the artefacts as and when they are brought in.
● Arrange for senior citizen(s) to visit the school and talk to the children about life when they were young. Discuss some of the changes that have taken place since those days, and ask the children to compare their lives now with those of their visitor(s) long ago.
● If possible, arrange a visit to a local museum, stately home or museum of childhood where the children can see displays of relevant artefacts. Some museums have loan schemes enabling schools to borrow artefacts for a few weeks. Emphasise to the children the importance of taking great care of such precious items.
● Local libraries may also arrange suitable talks for children with videos, pictures, workshops and so on. Arrange a visit if possible.

# ENGLISH ▶

**Speaking and listening**
● Talk to the children about the changes they have experienced in their lives, for example, in styles of clothing, toys, motor cars and so on. Bring in two or three interesting artefacts (such as a flat iron, or metal hair curling tongs which had to be heated on a fire/gas ring, and so on) and compare them with their modern equivalents. Show the artefacts one at a time to stimulate interest and let children guess what they are/how they are used. [1a-c, 2a-b, 3a-b]
● Read or tell stories and poems about the past. Talk about these with the children and encourage them all to join in class discussions. [1a-d, 2a-b, 3a-b]

**Reading**
● After reading some of the relevant poems/stories and discussing them, give the children opportunities to either re-read part of a story or to read a different poem/extract aloud to the other children. [1a-d, 2a-c, 3]
● Let the children work in groups to plan a story from the past. This could, of course, be the immediate past or five, ten, twenty or more years ago. If the latter, it will need careful planning and discussion with the children so that they are aware of historical facts, such as the evacuation of children at the outbreak of World War II, children at work in mines and factories, and so on. When ready, let the children tell/read their stories to the rest of the class. [1a-d, 2a-d, 3]

**Writing**
● Ask the children to draw/write imaginative stories about the past, for example, 'A Long Walk Home', 'A Day At School In 19__', 'My Journey Into The Past', and so on. Considerable discussion will be necessary before this is attempted, and the children must have some understanding of the period they are asked to write about. [1a, 1b, 1c, 2a-e, 3a, 3b]
● Help the children to produce factual writing about the relevant period in history, including information about fuels, clothing, transport, working lives, entertainments, social conditions etc. [1a-c, 2a-e, 3a-b]
● Make labels for the class museum, some giving brief information about artefacts on display. [1a-c, 2a-e, 3a-b]

# SCIENCE ▶

**Experimental and investigative science**
All activities below provide opportunities for experimental and investigative science.
● Discuss the materials used to make the artefact on display and what materials are used today. Let the children examine the flat iron, curling tongs, etc. and introduce the concept of natural materials such as wood, metal and glass and people-made materials like plastic, polythene and so on. [1a-e, 2a-b]

**Life processes and living things**
● Discuss the origins of coal, oil, wood, gas and elec-

tricity, and where they might be found. Talk about the effects on the environment of extracting/obtaining these and how the local or national landscape has changed over a period of time. Wherever possible, reinforce this discussion with books and 'then and now' pictures. [1a, 3a-c, 5a-b]

**Materials and their properties**
- Talk about the importance of fuels and how these have contributed to many changes that have taken place over a period of time, for example, transport, heating, lighting, etc. Ask the children to name the fuels they know and reinforce their knowledge of coal, electricity, gas, oil and wood. [1a-e, 2a-b]
- Arrange a display of natural/people-made materials.

Encourage children to help with the bringing in and organising of this display. Try to obtain wood, coal, metal, plastic, etc. and relate these to the class display of artefacts. Talk about the materials and their uses now and in the past. Ask the children to draw/write about selected materials – for example, are they hard or soft? Rough or smooth? Where are they obtained? [1a-e, 2a, 2b]

**Physical processes**
- Discuss homes of the past and the similarities and differences between then and now. Talk about the use of wood and coal for heating. What has taken its place? When talking about electricity and gas in the home discuss the importance of safety. [1a-c]

# MATHEMATICS ▶

All activities below provide opportunities for using and applying mathematics.

**Number**
**Using and applying mathematics**
- Make a 'Years' number line to fit behind the display of artefacts. This can be marked in sections of one, five or ten years and go back a hundred years if desired. Use the line for counting and mental arithmetic. [1a, 1c, 2a, 2b, 3a, 3c]

- Let the children discuss data they might record and then work individually and/or in small groups to design and construct graphs or diagrams for recording selected information. Statistics which might be recorded could include materials used to make artefacts on display, the most interesting artefact, the most useful artefact, etc. [1a, 1f, 5b]

# GEOGRAPHY ▶

**Geographical skills and places**
- If possible, obtain a large-scale map of the local area together with one showing the same area 20, 50, 100 or more years ago. These may be available from the Local Studies department of libraries. Talk about these with the children, and ask them if they can see ways in which the local area has changed over the years. [1a, 1b, 2, 3a-f]
- Prepare individual route maps for the children and let them use these on walks round the local area. Ask them to look for older buildings and/or changes currently taking place. Point out interesting features en route – street lamps old and new, new shop(s), pillar boxes, etc. On returning to school, ask the children to draw or write specific items in the correct place on their maps. [1a, 1b, 2, 3a-f]
- It may even be possible to obtain old trade journals or magazines which actually list details of homes and other buildings, street by street, including shops or other establishments that once were there and the names of families who lived on that street years ago. The children may be able to use this information to draw a sketch map or plan of what their street might have been like in the past. [1a, 1b, 2, 3f]
- Let the children observe photographs/pictures of the local area showing 'today and yesterday'. Discuss these and let the children talk about similarities and

differences. Try to obtain an aerial photograph for the children to study. [1a, 1b, 2, 3f]
- Give the children practice in saying/writing their home addresses and let them mark their houses on the large-scale map. Reinforce the name of the county in which they live and mark their town or village on a large wall map of Great Britain (or the nearest big town if appropriate).
- Discuss any changes that have taken place over a period of time, for example, are there more houses and/or roads? Have the shops changed? Help the children to record their findings. [1a, 1b, 2, 3a-f, 4, 5a-d]

**Thematic study**
- If the local area has grown since earlier maps, ask the class if they can suggest any reasons for this. Discuss work people might do – do some people travel to a larger city to work? Introduce the words 'commute' and 'commuter'. Help the children to begin to understand settlements and possible reasons for their decline or growth. [6a-c]
- Help children to recognise and name materials obtained from natural resources. Are any obtained from the local area? Where were they obtained from in the past? Were there any woods, a coal mine or a quarry in the area? [6a-c]

• Let the children debate their local area then and now, can they suggest any improvements for the future? What don't they like about the area at present? Let them write about this, giving individual opinions ask them to state whether they would prefer to live there in the past or today, giving reasons for their choice. Younger children can draw a picture of their choice and talk about their reasons. [6a-c]

# HISTORY ▶

### Areas of study (key elements 1–5)

• Tell children some historical events about the period being studied and place these in sequence. Let the children re-tell one or two events as picture stories, putting them in the correct historical sequence. [1a-b, 2, 3]

• Make a time-line from, say, a hundred years ago to today and arrange artefacts beneath the nearest 'time' slot on the line. [1a-b]

• Encourage children to listen carefully and discuss visitors' stories about the past. Talk about the difference between fact and fiction, and how factual stories can vary -liken this to the children's own reports of what happened at playtime, etc. [1a-b]

• Discuss all the artefacts that are brought into school. Talk about them one at a time, if possible, and let the children guess their use if these items are unusual. Children enjoy doing this, and it will stimulate their desire to bring in unusual exhibits. Compare them with other artefacts when discussing materials used in their manufacture. Let the children draw and/or write about selected items. [1a-b]

• Look at pictures and books of the past, as appropriate, and let children make deductions from what is shown in the pictures. Talk about the way that people lived at that time. [1a-b, 2, 3]

# ART ▶

### Investigating and making

• Use a variety of materials and techniques. Let the children create individual pictures of the period being studied, possibly linked to a story/sequence of events of that time.

• Let the children choose and examine selected artefacts, and help them to look at shape, form, etc., and then try to draw these.

• Suggest a wall frieze and discuss theme with children. Let them design, plan and make their picture. Give help and advice when required. A sequence picture could be created based on a theme of, say, flight or transport, clothes, etc.

### Knowledge and understanding

• Try to show children other examples of art in addition to pictures – perhaps wood carvings, metal design, etc. Hopefully, some examples of these might be brought in by the children for the classroom display. Look also for art in the local environment in the form of advertisements, statues and so on. Talk about these – do the children think art has changed?

• Look at some historical pictures depicting people, towns, villages, etc., and pictures of sculptures also depicting past/present art. Talk about these, encouraging children to give reasons for any preferences.

# MUSIC ▶

### Performing and composing

• Teach the children some songs from the period being studied. Reference books from the local library will assist with the selection of songs which were written during the period under consideration: a very popular wartime song, for example, was 'Run, Rabbit, Run'. Can they choose simple instruments to accompany one or two songs, and select when and how to play them.

• Take a theme from the past to the present day, for example, 'Flight'. Discuss the changes that have taken place from, say, man with wings on his arms through hot air balloons, bi-planes, jet aircraft, helicopters, Concorde, space rockets, etc. Can the children show these changes in patterns which will tell the story when put together? Can they compose a piece of music, using simple instruments, to tell the story? Let them record their compositions and play them to the other children.

- Let the children learn singing games, if appropriate, and allow time to try some of them.

**Listening and appraising**
- Talk with children about the songs they have learned. Are they different from today's popular songs? If so, how? Discuss pace, timbre, dynamics and so on, as well perhaps as the advent of synthesisers and other 'new' instruments.

- Select some music relevant to the period being studied and let the children listen to it from time to time. If marches and/or waltzes are included in the repertoire, talk about the various rhythms and any effect that the music might have – does the music make the children want to move, dance, tap their feet, etc?

# P.E. ▶

**Games**
- Let the children play some traditional games from the period being studied, including singing games.

# HEALTH EDUCATION ▶

- Talk about the importance of taking care when using various fuels. Discuss one fuel at a time, and mention any precautions that must be taken when it is being used.
- If studying a period of time between fifty and a hundred years ago, discuss hygiene (or the lack of it) in those days. Tell the children about any advances in medicine which may have taken place between then and now.
- Talk about the importance of keeping clean, washing hands after visiting the toilet, keeping homes clean, food hygiene and so on.

**Blueprints links**
**Art Key Stage 1:** many activities and copymasters on art in history; **Art Resource Bank:** many copymasters on art in history; **Health Education Key Stage 1:** topic on growing up and copymasters 11, 14, 20, 21, 94–95; **History Key Stage 1:** complete resource on the past; **Infant Teacher's Resource Bank:** copymasters 126–130 (then and now); **Poetry Book:** copymasters 11, 42–44; **Religious Education Key Stage 1:** copymasters 11, 66; **Second Key Stage 1 Topics Book:** Time copymaster 7; **Topics Key Stage 1:** topic on dinosaurs; **Writing 5–8:** many copymasters (see index).

# TREES

## ENGLISH

- Explore trees with all senses
- Describe a favourite tree
- Listen to and read tree stories, poems and rhymes
- Learn oral instructions in order to protect trees
- Compile a tree dictionary
- Label posters and pictures and displays
- Read non-fiction reference material
- Write words about a favourite tree
- Write up results of field investigations
- Write stories about trees

## ENVIRONMENTAL EDUCATION

- Learn about tropical rain forests
- Consider the value of trees
- Plant a tree

## GEOGRAPHY

- Make a variety of tree pictures based on observations and collections
- Make a 'tree life' collage
- Make leaf prints
- Press leaves
- Make wall hangings
- Construct items from wood
- Study beautiful trees and look at well-known works of art

## DESIGN AND TECHNOLOGY

- Identify needs for, design, plan and make objects from wood
- Evaluate wood as design material
- Make and use a database(s)

## R.E.

- Consider the place of trees in world religions and stories

## GEOGRAPHY

- Learn about trees and fruits from distant lands
- Relate to weather and vegetation
- Investigate wood as a resource and global industry
- Consider the effects of removing trees
- Plant trees to enhance the community

## MATHEMATICS

- Use mathematics to investigate various aspects of trees
- Count with and estimate tree fruits and seeds
- Calculate chlorophyll loss
- Investigate tree shapes
- Represent data pictorially and on databases

## SCIENCE

- Observe trees in different seasons
- Make regular repeated observations
- Predict changes in trees
- Measure trees
- Observe and explain changes
- Test predictions on habits
- Plant and grow seeds
- Name tree parts
- Find out basic needs of trees
- Classify and identify trees
- Learn to take care of trees
- Investigate habitats
- Research life in/on trees
- Research uses of wood
- Consider wood as a resource

## IDEAS BANK
General starting points: Suggestions for programmes of study of core and foundation subjects relating to topic, and links with cross-curricular themes and R.E.

## STARTING POINTS
● Observe a tree or trees in the school grounds. Whatever the season, this can be rewarding: see the leaves of summer, the fruits and leaf colour changes in autumn; the stark shapes, bark and evergreen leaves of winter; and the buds and blossom of springtime.
● Go out on a field visit to a woodland or forest. Get a 'feel' for a place where many trees grow together, and study other forms of life there.
● Bring a collection of leaves, fruits or tree seeds into the classroom to generate initial discussion.
● Make a collection of stories, poems, rhymes and pictures about trees.

# SCIENCE ▶

### Experimental and investigative science
All activities marked with an asterisk below provide opportunities for experimental and investigative science.
● *Go out and observe a tree or trees – in the school grounds, park or woodland. Discuss the shape and parts of the tree that can be seen (leaves, bark, flowers, fruit, etc.) Note the season of the year in which the observation is taking place. [1a-c, 2a-c, 3a-f]
● *Make a series of related observations: visit the same tree/trees on a regular basis. Note subtle changes in leaves, flowers, fruits, or life living on or visiting the tree. [1a-c, 2a-c, 3a-f]
● *Make predictions as to how parts of the tree/trees observed above may change in the next few days or weeks, and test hypotheses. [1a-c, 2a-c, 3a-f]
● *Undertake measurements of tree and tree parts (height if possible, girth, leaves, fruits, etc.), selecting suitable instruments for this. [1a-c, 2a-c, 3a-f]
● *Observe significant tree changes, for example, change in leaf colour, falling leaves, opening of buds, development of fruit, and so on. Describe what is happening, and provide simple explanations of why. [2a-c, 3a-c]
● *Make predictions in late summer or early autumn about whether certain specimens will lose their leaves. Test predictions later, and discuss upon what basis predictions were made. [1a-c, 2a-c, 3a-f]
● *Plant tree seeds of various sorts, and perhaps in varying places/conditions. Observe and measure growth. [1a-c, 2a-c, 3a-f]

### Life processes and living things
● *Help children to learn the names of tree parts, preferably by direct observation in the field. Key words at this stage are tree, trunk, bark, roots, branches, flowers, buds, fruits, seeds. [1a, 3a, 3b, 3c, 4b, 5a, 5b]
● *Help them to appreciate that a tree is a large member of the plant kingdom and that trees bear flowers, which vary greatly from one species to another. [1a, 3a, 3b, 3c, 4b, 5a, 5b]
● *Discuss and research the needs of trees to keep them alive and healthy – notably nourishment, water, sunlight. [3a]

(NOTE: At this stage, children will no doubt appreciate that trees obtain food from the soil – with older children, begin to help them understand that trees can also make food in their green leaves from sunlight – thus this is essential.)

● *Begin attempts at tree classification -discuss differences in size and shape of leaves, appearance of flowers, fruits and seeds and habits (i.e. whether leaves die and fall in autumn or not). [3b]
● *Pursue classification by helping children to identify individual tree species, also to sort trees into basic groups such as broadleaf, conifer; evergreen, deciduous (which of course are not the same). [3b, 3c, 4b, 5a, 5b]
● Learn to use simple identification keys. [3b, 3c, 4b, 5a, 5b]
● Discuss the need to take care of trees: help children to appreciate that when trees are cut down, changes in the environment result that can affect our world, its plants and animals (relate to Environmental Education activities). [5a, 5b]
● *Consider the localities (habitats) of trees: help children to appreciate that trees can grow singly (in gardens, school grounds) or in groups such as in woods and forests. All have various forms of life such as birds, animals and insects associated with them. [4b, 5a, 5b]
● *Study a single tree or group of trees in order to identify and record forms of animal, bird and insect life associated with it – sketch and identify associated species; also other forms of plant life such as mosses and lichens living in association with the tree(s). In other words, establish a tree or trees as a living community or habitat, with a rich variety of associated life. [1a, 3a, 3b, 3c, 4b, 5a, 5b]

### Materials and their properties
● *Discuss wood as a basic raw material obtained from trees, together with its properties and uses. [1a-e]
● *Undertake a sub-topic on uses of wood in our lives, perhaps considering whether the use of trees for material is essential or a luxury. [1c, 1d, 1e, 2a]
● *Discuss and research the differences between wood as a natural common resource, and other products used in everyday life which are made from raw materials. [1a-e, 2a-b]

# ENVIRONMENTAL EDUCATION ▶

- Pursue a sub-topic on tropical rain forests, researching and discussing the causes and consequences of deforestation, life in a rain forest, and the need to conserve the world's rain forest areas.
- Help children to appreciate why we should take care of trees in our own neighbourhoods – i.e. for their own beauty and intrinsic value, and the life which they support.
- Plant a tree or trees to enhance your school grounds.

# ENGLISH ▶

## Speaking and listening

- Talk about trees, preferably whilst in the field observing them – their shape, texture, beauty, colourings, etc. Encourage the children to respond to explorations of trees using all their senses. [1a-d, 2a, 2b, 3a, 3b]
- Let the children select a favourite tree well known to them, perhaps in their gardens, school grounds or park. Ask them to describe it to the rest of the class and explain why it is very special. [1a-d, 2a, 2b, 3a, 3b]
- Make a collection of published stories, poems and rhymes about trees to read out loud on a regular basis. Use these as a basis for discussion and suggesting ideas to follow up in the field. [1a-d, 2a, 2b, 3a, 3b]
- Give precise oral instructions about working in the field so that children understand clearly what they have to do and will cause no harm to the trees they are studying. [1c, 2a, 2b]

## Reading

- Display a set of pictures or posters of trees on the classroom wall, with simple labels appended explaining their names and perhaps their parts. [1b, 1c, 2a, 2b]
- Help the children to compile an illustrated class dictionary of trees and related subjects. Words and definitions can of course be as numerous and complex as you wish, depending on the ability of the children. Let the children read this as part of their classroom research material. [1a, 1b, 2a, 2b, 2d, 3]

- Provide a reading corner of stories, poems and rhymes about trees for the children to access freely. Their own written poems and stories can be added for others to share. [1a-d, 2a-d, 3]
- Encourage the reading of and engage children in research from non-fiction material about trees and related subjects. [1b, 1c, 2a-d, 3]

## Writing

- Suggest that children draw a picture of their favourite tree, and write one or two key words which best describe it – perhaps its name or key adjectives. [1a-c, 2a-e, 3b]
- Produce coherent writing, relating to field and classroom investigations of tree and tree parts, explaining findings and feelings about trees. [1a-c, 2a-e, 3a-b]
- Compose and write stories about trees, or life associated with trees. Individuals could write their own imaginative stories, or compose class-based writing on such topics as 'A Year In The Life Of The Fir Tree', 'The Oak Tree's Visitors', 'My Life Beneath A Silver Birch'. [1a-c, 2a-e, 3a-b]
- Suggest that the children write accounts about trees which people have decided to chop down, explaining their feelings and reasons for and against this action. [1a-c, 2a-e, 3a-b]
- Write labels for parts of trees (leaves, twigs, fruits, seeds, etc.) displayed in the classroom. [1a-c, 2a-e, 3b]

# GEOGRAPHY ▶

## Geographical skills and places

- Use photographs, secondary resource material and perhaps the plants themselves (for example, a rubber tree) to help children learn about trees in distant lands. Trees can be used as a reference point for helping children to appreciate differences in vegetation and climate, and to relate these to their own homelands. [1c, 2, 3a, 3b, 3e, 3f, 4, 5a-d]
- Visit your local supermarket and observe or obtain fruits from trees from distant lands. As above, use as reference points for developing an understanding of

differences between the home and distant environments. [1c, 2, 3e, 3f, 5a-d]
- Following on from the above research and discuss contrasting weather conditions in different parts of the world and relate to the types and habits of trees which live there. [1c, 2, 3e, 3f, 5b, 5c]

## Geographical skills and thematic study

- Identify wood as being a key resource obtained from trees throughout the world. [1a-c, 2, 3b, 3f, 6a-c]
- Research how wood is obtained and which nations

are the leading producers of the world's timber supplies. [1b, 1c, 2, 3e, 3f, 6b, 6c]
● Find out where the UK obtains most of its timber for manufacture and identify a range of goods made from timber of various sorts. [1c, 2, 3e, 3f, 6a-c]
● Identify the effects on the environments of the world's forests of removing trees: relate to Environmen-

tal Education and sub-topic on tropical rain forests. [1c, 2, 3f, 6a-c]
● Plant a tree in your school grounds and/or observe tree planting schemes in the local community. Describe and discuss orally or in writing how such activities are designed to improve the environment. [1a-c, 2, 6a-c]

# DESIGN AND TECHNOLOGY

## Design and technology capability
● Use knowledge and results of investigations about trees to identify opportunities for classroom construction of items with available wood supplies. [1a-c, 2a-c]

## Designing skills
● Discuss ideas, make pictures, drawings and models to develop design proposals, identifying why the proposed item should be made, and why wood is a suitable construction material. [3a-f]

## Making skills and knowledge and understanding
● Use available wood types to make simple items according to design as discussed. [4a-d]
● Discuss the differences between hardwoods and softwoods, and the appropriateness of these for specific

construction activities. Discuss the types of wood available in the classroom. Select appropriate resources to construct items according to design. [4a-f]
● Having constructed items with wood(s) available, discuss how satisfied the children are with their technological activities, and the appropriateness or limitations of the woods used. Relate to a developing understanding of the properties of hard and soft woods. [4f]

## Information technology
● Enter data collected in the field (tree sizes, number of various species, life forms associated with tree habitats, etc) onto a computer database. Access information when required. [1a-c, 2a-c, 3a-c]
● Discuss the use of information stored on a database, compared with other methods by which children have recorded it. [1a-c]

# MATHEMATICS

## Using and applying mathematics
All activities below provide opportunities for using and applying mathematics.

## Number
● Use tree fruits such as acorns or conkers as objects for counting, at the same time developing awareness of the size, shape and differences between fruits. [1a, 1c, 1e, 1f, 2a-c, 3c, 5b]
● Make estimates, for example, of the number of trees in a park or woodland. Check results by counting as accurately as possible. [1a, 1b, 1c, 1e, 1f, 2a-c, 3c, 3e, 5b]
● Sort trees and tree parts using carefully selected criteria (for example, size, habits – deciduous, evergreen, family, name etc.) Enter information into a database and access it as required. [1f, 5a-b]
● Record the above information on a range of graphs/pictorial representations, for display, discussion and future reference. [5a-b]

## Shape, space and measures
● Examine colour loss in fallen autumn leaves. Help

the children to find ways of calculating the area of chlorophyll (green colour) that has been lost from leaves you have collected, perhaps by drawing around leaves and areas of their colours on squared paper. Use a symbol to stand for the area of chlorophyll lost that you are trying to find out about. [1a, 1c, 2c, 4a]
● Stand a distance away from trees and look at their whole shape – in different seasons of the year. Talk about the shape made by their crown (branches) in the sky. Consider whether any trees display symmetry. [1a, 2a, 2c]
● Make collections of leaves, fruits and seeds (from the ground, without damaging the trees). Discuss and identify their shapes, as far as this is possible. Compare and order them without measuring. [1a, 1c, 2a, 2c]
● Following on from the above, investigate which trees have single fruits (conkers), which have paired seeds (sycamore wings) and which have fruits with multiple seeds (cones). Similarly, discuss simple (oak) and more complex leaf shapes made of multiple leaflets (horse chestnut). [1a, 1c, 2a, 2c, 4a]

# R.E.

• Consider the significance of trees in some of the well-known stories from world religions, and their place in religious beliefs and festivals (for example, from Christianity). Tell of the use of palm branches on the first Palm Sunday, the fact that Christ was crucified on a wooden cross (legend tells it was from the Dogwood tree), and you may like to research and describe the Jewish festival of trees.

*Background information:*
On the fifteenth day of the Hebrew month Shevat comes the New Year festival for trees called Tu B' Shevat or Rosh Hashana L'ilanot, meaning 'New Year for trees'. This festival is celebrated by Jews world-wide as a planting day for trees.

# ART

### Investigating and making
• Use discarded items collected from beneath trees (bits of bark, leaves, fruits, seeds, etc.) to make collage pictures of trees and woodland scenes. Pay close attention to selecting colours, textures and shapes to create a pleasing effect.
• Make sketches and paintings of various tree features, from observations from direct experience outdoors.
• After a visit to a park or woodland, ask the children to paint or use other media to make a representation of their favourite tree and to explain how they have tried to show its beauty or special features in the picture.
• Make a large wall collage displaying animal and plant life associated with a tree or woodland.

• Make leaf prints on material. Embellish with needlecraft techniques to create permanent wall hangings.
• Press fallen leaves and mount on stiff card. Cover with transparent adhesive material for longer-lasting pictures.
• Craft objects and images out of wood (relate to technology activities).

### Knowledge and understanding
• On a field visit, look for and share views on trees that are particularly beautiful or aesthetically pleasing in some way.
• Collect and share with the children pictures of trees by well-known artists for discussion of colour, mood, etc. If possible, visit an art gallery for this purpose.

### Blueprints links
**Art Key Stage 1:** activities 29, 147, copymasters 16, 71, 74; **Art Resource Bank:** copymasters 33, 62; **Christmas Art and Craft:** tree decorations; **Distant Places:** New Zealand copymaster 6, Brazil copymasters 5–6; **Easter:** Eastertime copymaster 2; **Early Years Songs and Rhymes:** pages 6, 18, 23, 24, 50, 73, 96; **Environmental Education Key Stage 1:** complete topic on trees; **Festivals:** copymaster page 107; **Geography Key Stage 1:** copymasters 112, 114; **Health**

**Education Key Stage 1:** copymaster 82; **Infant Geography Resource Bank:** copymasters 57–60 (making wooden furniture), copymasters 101–102 (rain forests); **Infant Teacher's Resource Bank:** copymaster 135 (common trees); **Poetry Book:** section on trees, copymasters 61–4; **Religious Education Key Stage 1:** copymaster 87; **Seasonal Activities:** Spring copymasters 4, 11, Spring template 6, Autumn copymasters 5–7, Autumn templates 4–6, Winter copymaster 11.

# MINIBEASTS

## ENGLISH

- Tell stories, poems, rhymes about minibeasts
- Discuss creatures studied
- Listen to important instructions
- Have an oral quiz
- Read and discuss stories, poems, rhymes
- Prepare questions to answer
- Prepare information cards
- Write identification cards
- Undertake formal writing about all observations and investigations
- Compose imaginary stories
- Write about fictitious creatures
- Write accurate labels for creatures in the classroom

## ENVIRONMENTAL EDUCATION

- Consider the balance of nature
- Investigate decomposition
- Recognise the need to take care of minibeasts

## ART

- Construct food chain mobiles
- Draw/paint from observations
- Represent body patterns
- Represent body textures
- Make pictures showing symmetry
- Make 3-D models
- Create imaginary minibeasts

## DESIGN AND TECHNOLOGY

- Research classroom housing needs
- Design and construct housing, evaluate results
- Enter and retrieve minibeast data on a computer

## R.E.

- Tell the O.T. Bible story of the locust plague of Egypt
- Consider the hazards of invertebrates
- Debate the importance of minibeasts

**MINIBEASTS**

## GEOGRAPHY

- Study minibeasts from distant lands
- Obtain and rear foreign species
- Consider differences between native and foreign specimens
- Relate differences to climate, vegetation, etc.

## MATHEMATICS

- Do body part calculations
- Estimate sizes
- Measure the speed of movement
- Use symbols for body part numbers
- Compare and order sizes
- Discuss and identify body shapes
- Observe and record symmetry
- Sort invertebrates
- Record data on graphs
- Create databases

## P.E.

- Move like invertebrates
- Compose a minibeast dance

## SCIENCE

- Make detailed observations
- Investigate and predict behaviour
- Collect creatures for classroom study
- Design fair tests to investigate habits and behaviour
- Classify minibeasts
- Identify individual members of classes
- House and rear one or more species in the classroom
- Study food chains and webs
- Consider long-term rearing

## IDEAS BANK
General starting points: Suggestions for programmes of study of core and foundation subjects relating to topic, and links with cross-curricular themes and R.E.

## STARTING POINTS
• Go out into the school grounds and undertake a minibeast hunt. Collect specimens for close observation and further investigation in the classroom.
• Order, obtain and rear a selection of one or more non-native minibeasts.
• Read a story associated with minibeasts such as 'The Very Hungry Caterpillar'.

# SCIENCE ▶

### Experimental and investigative science
All activities below provide opportunities for experimental and investigative science.

### Life processes and living things
• Observe minibeasts in their natural habitats: make a series of related observations of such factors as size, shape, movement of a range of invertebrate creatures in a range of habitats. [1a-b, 4b, 5a-b]
• Help the children to suggest ideas and make predictions about invertebrate behaviour (for example, what will happen if the weather changes or the seasons change). In due course, compare what is observed with what was expected or predicted. [1a-b, 4b, 5a-b]
• Carefully collect one or more invertebrates for classroom study, making sure that they are returned to their natural habitat as soon as short-term studies are complete. Observe them closely, for example, studying body parts, measuring, and observing feeding and day/night time behaviour. [1a-b, 4b, 5a-b]
• Design fair tests to verify conclusions – for example, to see which moves more speedily across a certain distance, a millipede or a snail. [1b, 4b]
• Help children to understand that minibeasts belong to the group of creatures called invertebrates in the animal kingdom: they are different from many other animals because they have no backbone. [4b]
• Observe and discuss the characteristics of invertebrates in general, and those of key invertebrate families. Help children to be able to distinguish between classes or families of creatures by observation of body parts (insects, slugs and snails, spiders, worms, etc.) and to identify individual creatures. [4b]
• Select a particular class of minibeast (for example, insect) or member of that class (such as ants, caterpillars) for in-depth study. Provide appropriate classroom housing for short-term keeping or rearing. Through carefully designed observations and investigations, find out more about conditions that are necessary to sustain life. [1b, 4b, 5a-b]

(NOTE: It should be remembered that invertebrates are living creatures and must be treated with care and respect at all times. No investigation should have the potential to cause harm or stress, and creatures should be returned to their natural habitat as soon as possible, unless adequate long-term classroom care is planned and feasible.)

• Consider the place of invertebrates in simple food chains and food webs. Extend your studies of what foods they eat and sources of their food, to thinking about who eats them. [1b, 4b, 5a-b]
• Set up an appropriate area for long-term rearing of a chosen minibeast. Consult specialist books on the subject and obtain specimens from a reputable supplier of biological material. Life and living processes can thus be studied in depth as complete life-cycles (metamorphoses) can be observed. Suitable creatures include caterpillars of moths and butterflies, ants, snails, worms, beetles and spiders. A range of exciting foreign invertebrates is also available (link with geography activities). [1a-b, 4b, 5a-b]

# GEOGRAPHY ▶

### Geographical skills and places
• Use invertebrates from distant lands as the basis for finding out about foreign places. Investigate invertebrate life from information books on other lands and consider keeping some of these creatures. Consult specialist reading and suppliers; obtain and rear one or more specimens such as locusts from desert lands, stick insects from India or Australia, giant snails from Africa, giant hissing cockroaches or millipedes from tropical lands, foreign moths or butterflies. Consider similarities and differences between these and native counterparts in terms of size, colouring, food, movement, habits, etc. [1c, 2, 3e, 3f, 4]
• Continue the above activity to relate observations to differences in climate, and hence vegetation, food sources, etc. [1c, 2, 3e, 3f, 4, 5b, 5c]

# MATHEMATICS

**Using and applying mathematics**
All activities below provide opportunities for using and applying mathematics.

**Number**
- Focus on counting body parts of one or more minibeasts closely observed in the field or classroom. Design a range of tasks to give practice in addition, subtraction, multiplication and division – for example, how many legs on one insect, on 3 insects, on 6 insects, how many wings on 6 moths, etc. [1a, 1c, 1d, 1e, 2a-c, 3a-e, 4a-d]
- Use symbols to stand for a number of invertebrate body parts (x legs, y antennae, etc.) Count parts and verify number. [1a, 1e]
- Sort a set of selected and observed minibeasts according to criteria chosen, such as number and variety of body parts. [5a-b]
- Draw graphs to record data collected as a result of field and classroom observations of minibeasts, for example, of sizes or speed of movement. [5b]

- Create a database to record observations of number and size of creatures and their body parts: access information. [5b]

**Shape, space and measures**
- Compare the size of various creatures observed and order them, without measuring. [4a]
- Discuss and identify shapes as observed on minibeasts (for example, spiral shell, cylindrical body, oval thorax, etc.) [2a]
- Observe and record symmetry as displayed in creatures such as butterflies, moths, millipedes, etc. [2a-c]
- Estimate the size of invertebrates observed and reared; check results with familiar units of measurement. [4a-b]
- Measure the speed of movement of selected species by timing movement across squared paper; compare speeds of individual creatures of the same or different classes. [4a-b]

# ART

**Investigating and making**
- Construct food chain mobiles: paint and cut out invertebrates and other plants/animals linked in their food chains. Join together with string or ribbon in correct sequence and suspend from ceiling.
- Draw, paint or make collages of minibeasts as a result of direct observations, both in the field and at close quarters in the classroom.
- Explore and artistically represent patterns displayed on invertebrates, such as spirals on snails, colour symmetry on butterflies, spot patterns on ladybirds and so on.

- Explore and recreate, using collage and needlecraft techniques, various textures of invertebrates – the slimy slug, the slippery worm, the shiny beetle, etc.
- Make three-dimensional models of minibeasts studied. Display against a backcloth of writing and two-dimensional art work.
- Design and create pictures of imaginary minibeasts such as the giant hissing slug, the ferocious yellow caterpillar, and so on. Base discussion and designs on vivid imaginative extension of actual observations.

# ENGLISH

**Speaking and listening**
- Tell stories, poems and rhymes for the children to listen and respond to which focus on minibeasts, such as 'Incey Wincey Spider', 'Ladybird, Ladybird', and 'The Very Hungry Caterpillar'. [1a-d]
- Engage in as much structured discussion as possible about creatures studied, encouraging children to describe, ask and answer questions. [1b, 1c, 2a, 2b, 3]
- Ensure that children listen to instructions about care and safety when dealing with minibeasts, relating both to the creatures and to themselves. [1c, 2b, 3]
- Organise an oral quiz where the children play a question and answer game to identify minibeasts. [1a-d, 2a-b, 3]

**Reading**
- Following the reading out loud of various published stories and rhymes about minibeasts, encourage the children to re-read this material themselves and to comment upon whether the minibeasts portrayed are like those observed in real life. [1a, 1c, 1d, 2a-d, 3]
- Devise a set of questions about specific creatures studied for the children to research and answer, using carefully selected information sources and reference books. [1b, 1c, 2a-d, 3]
- Produce a set of cards presenting simple information about a range of minibeasts (one card for each creature) and perhaps another set bearing the names of these creatures. Let the children read the descriptions and match them with the appropriate name. [1b, 1c, 2a-d, 3]

### Writing
● Suggest that children make a card or painting for each minibeast observed, bearing a picture of it along with its name. [1a-c, 2a, 2d, 2e, 3b]
● Produce factual writing related to observations and investigations of minibeasts studied in the field and reared in the classroom. [1a-c, 2a-e, 3]
● Compose imaginary stories about events in the life of a minibeast based on the habits of real creatures observed. [1a-c, 2a-e, 3]

● Compose stories about fictitious invertebrate creatures. With younger children, perhaps titles may be suggested to inspire imaginative thinking, such as 'Adventures Of The Purple Spotted Billipede', 'Tales of Inverty: the friendliest life in the ground.' [1a-c, 2a-e, 3]
● Write accurate labels for your classroom invertebrates, providing not only their names but also important information about handling, feeding and general care. [1a-c, 2a-e, 2]

# P.E.

### P.E.
● Encourage the children to move like invertebrates, perhaps to the accompaniment of your own music/sounds: glide like a slug, wriggle like a worm, leap like a locust, amble like a centipede, flutter like a butterfly. Compose a minibeast 'dance'.

# DESIGN AND TECHNOLOGY

### Design and technology capability
● Research the practical needs of invertebrates and identify specifications for appropriate classroom housing. [1a-c, 2a-c]

### Designing skills
● Talk about needs as identified, and make appropriate designs for housing invertebrates indoors. [1a-f]

### Making skills and knowledge and understanding
● Select and use appropriate materials to construct housing suitable for keeping one or more invertebrates in the classroom on a short-term basis. [1a-c]

● Discuss the results of your housing construction project, deciding how adequate it is, how satisfied you are with the results, how long it will last, and what limitations there are, if any. [1f]

### Information technology
● Let children enter data collected about invertebrates (for example, how many of each kind observed, how many body parts, feeding needs, habitats, etc.) into a computer database. Give other children practice in retrieving this information. [1a-c, 2a-c, 3a-c]

# ENVIRONMENTAL EDUCATION

● Discuss and observe the role of invertebrate creatures in the balance of nature: their role in decomposition, and thus their great importance to the natural world.

● Following on from the above, help children to appreciate the need to take as much care of minibeasts as any other living creature, and also to preserve their natural habitats.

# R.E.

● Tell the Old Testament story about Moses and the plagues of Egypt, including the plague of locusts (Exodus 10, verses 12–15). Discuss the extent to which minibeasts can be dangerous or hazardous to the world.
● Following on from the above, organise a class debate on 'invertebrates: friend or foe', presumably concluding with the important message (linked to environmental education work) that they are an essential part of our world, and creatures of which we must take care.

### Blueprints links
Art Key Stage 1: activities 153, 156, 159, 237; Early Years Songs and Rhymes: pages 7, 15, 43, 49; Environmental Education Key Stage 1: topic on ponds; Geography Key Stage 1: copymaster 70 (wildlife survey); Infant Geography Resource Bank: copymaster 85 (pond creatures); Infant Teacher's Resource Bank: copymaster 117 (Picture of pond creatures); Religious Education Key Stage 1: copymaster 77; Seasonal Activities: Summer copymasters 9 and 10, Summer templates 4–6, Autumn Copymaster 4, Winter copymaster 7.

# PEOPLE

**ENGLISH**

- Investigate the human voice
- Listen to other languages
- Read and write about various people
- Communicate feelings about people
- Write descriptions of people

**ENVIRONMENTAL EDUCATION**

- Consider human impact on the global environment
- Consider conservation
- Investigate population growth and impact

**MUSIC**

- Listen to music from a variety of cultures

**ART**

- Make a 'Human race' frieze
- Make pictures of people of the past
- Look at artists' work about people

**CITIZENSHIP**

- Consider the role of people as citizens in a community

**MATHEMATICS**

- Do 'people' sums
- Investigate population statistics
- Handle and interpret data

**R.E.**

- Consider population control
- Consider similarities and differences between people
- Tell the Bible story of the first people

**GEOGRAPHY**

- Find out about people in different parts of the UK
- Research the lives, interests and activities of people in the local area
- Interview people
- Collect data from people from afar
- Collect pictures of people from around the world
- Research people's journeys, home moves and work
- Find out how people can change their environments
- Discuss whether such changes are good or bad

**HISTORY**

- Construct family trees
- Research relatives' lives
- Read and find out about people of the past
- Learn about past people through artefacts
- Compare present day and past household goods
- Read historic stories about people
- Research a variety of historic sources
- Interview people about the past
- Observe photographs of people in the past

**SCIENCE**

- Do detailed observations of each other
- Monitor human activity during a day
- Learn about human body parts
- Compare human, animal and plant parts
- Research basic human life processes
- Research the impact of human life on plants and animals
- Consider human impact on the environment, including destructive impacts

**IDEAS BANK**
General starting points: Suggestions for programmes of study of core and foundation subjects relating to topic, and links with cross-curricular themes and R.E.

**STARTING POINTS**
● Make a collection of pictures of people from around the world, gathered from magazines, tourist brochures etc.

● Go out into your town or neighbourhood shopping centre, railway station, or similar place where the children can sit and observe the 'world going by'. Watch people going about their everyday business.
● Ask the children to bring photographs of themselves and their close relations to school, as well as historic photographs of people in their families.
● Select an individual person. Interview them about their life, home, work, interests, etc.

# SCIENCE ▶

**Experimental and investigative science**
All activities below provide opportunities for experimental and investigative science.

**Life processes and living things**
● Let the children observe each other during various activities of the day (working in the classroom, out at play, doing P.E. etc.). Talk and write about what they are doing or activities that they are engaged in. [1a-b, 2a, 2f, 4a-b]
● Extend the above by pairing the children, and asking them to monitor the activities and actions of their partner throughout a school day, reporting on what is observed, recording results and in subsequent observations, predicting likely actions and behaviour. [1a-b, 2a, 2b, 2c, 2f, 4a-b]
● Look at pictures of the human body and of a human skeleton. Learn the names of the main external parts. [2a]
● Discuss the differences between the body parts and activities of humans, and those of other

members of the animal kingdom; also, the differences between humans and plants. [1b, 2b, 2c, 2e, 2f, 3a-c, 4a-b, 5a-b]
● Talk about and research the basic life processes that are essential to human beings, such as feeding, breathing, reproducing, communicating, moving, etc. [2b, 2c, 2e, 2f]
● Discuss the results of observations suggested earlier and relate to essential life processes, for example, the need to eat, communicate, move, go to the toilet, etc. [1b, 2b, 2c, 2e, 2f, 4a-b]
● Research the impact that human life has on plants and animals; for example, pursue a study of the place of human life in food chains, or study of sports such as hunting, shooting and fishing. [1b, 2a-f, 3a-c, 4b, 5a-b]
● Consider ways in which human life can have a significant impact on the environment, thus affecting plants and animals, for example, by removing forests and hedgerows, turning areas of countryside into locations for towns and industry. [5a-b]

# HISTORY ▶

**Areas of study (Key Elements 1-5)**
● Investigate children's roots. Help each child to work out a family tree, going as far back through the generations as possible, thus placing people in their families in sequence. Exercise sensitivity and discretion in the case of single parent families or others who may consider your investigations to be intrusive. [1a-b]
● Talk about and research the lives of some of the people on your class family trees (or focus on one or more members of your own family). Through discovering more about the ways of life of these people (food, clothing, jobs, etc.), identify differences between past and present times. [1a-b]
● Read stories about people of the past. Discuss these, and help the children to place events of the stories in sequence. [2, 3]
● Make a collection of objects and artefacts that would commonly have been found in people's homes in days gone by. Discuss what these tell us about life in the past, and discuss whether similar objects are in use today. [1a-b]
● Following on from the above, talk about things

commonly used in everyday life by people today. Discuss those items that we take for granted that have not always been available even in the comparatively recent past, such as Compact Disc players and computers. [1a-b]
● Read stories about people of the past, both real and fictional characters. Discuss these, helping children to begin to appreciate the differences between historic fact and fiction, and between facts and points of view. [1b, 2, 3]
● Use a variety of sources to find out about the lives of people of the past, for example, reference books, parish records, school log books, newspapers, films, video and audio tapes, etc. [1b, 2, 3]
● Use people themselves to help children find out about and answer questions about the past: invite elderly people into school for structured interviews and discussion about specific events or themes relating to their past. [1a-b, 3]
● Ask the children to bring to school photographs of their present family and relatives who are no longer alive. Use them in association with building up family trees. [1a-b]

# GEOGRAPHY

**Geographical skills and places**
- Focus on people who live in different parts of the UK. Identify common aspects of people's lives, but also differences in the lives of inhabitants of contrasting localities – for example, in a large city and a rural community. [1a-c, 2, 3a-f, 4, 5a-d]
- Observe and find out more about the lives of people in your local area – perhaps observe them going about their daily lives in a busy street or railway station – or do surveys to find out how people spend their time, or where they work or live. [1a-c, 2, 3a-f, 4, 5a-d]
- Select an individual person or people in your local area to interview – either by questionnaire or by personal visit. Find out about their home, work, interests, involvement in the local community, etc. [1a]
- Make arrangements for similar data collection from people in contrasting areas of the UK or overseas – perhaps by sending questionnaires to link schools, or forming pen friend links. Compare data with that collected from people in your local area. Suggest reasons for differences. [1a-c, 2, 3a-f, 4, 5a-d]
- Make a collection of pictures of people from around the world, perhaps from magazines and tourist brochures. Use this simply to make a colourful display/montage, helping children to appreciate different appearances of people from other lands, or use them as a basis for specific focus on people in one contrasting nation or continent. [1a-c, 2, 3c, 3f, 4, 5a-d]

**Geographical skills and thematic study**
- Conduct a survey or sub-topic on journeys people make. Perhaps interview people at a bus or railway station, or ask people to list all journeys made by whatever means over a period of time. Explore reasons for journeys, length of time taken and mode of transport. [1a-c, 2, 3a-f, 6a-c]
- Survey members of your class or school to find out where they live and how long they have lived there. In instances where people have moved, find out from where and why the move(s) took place. As before, such questioning should be done with discretion. [1a-c, 2, 3d, 6a-c]
- Survey members of your class, school or community to find out what kinds of work adults are engaged in (clearly to be treated with sensitivity if people are unemployed). Relate results to a study of the location of business, industries and other buildings in your local area. [1a-c, 2, 3d, 6a-c]
- Discuss the many ways in which people can change the natural environment, for example, by building on it, making roads and railways, mining, removing forests and hedgerows, etc. [1a-c, 2, 6a-c]
- Look for field evidence in your local area which demonstrates how people have changed or are changing the environment in some substantial way. Ask the children whether they think the change(s) are for better or worse, and who will benefit. [1a-c, 2, 6a-c]

# ENVIRONMENTAL EDUCATION

**Environmental education**
- Extend the above activities by considering one or more of the substantial impacts that people are having on the world as a whole. Topics for specific focus could include rain forest destruction (causes and consequences), global warming (the role of people in the depletion of the ozone layer), pollution (of land, air or oceans).
- Introduce the concept of conservation and investigate ways in which people may act in order to help protect our planet rather than have a damaging impact upon it (perhaps focusing on one or more areas of human activity).
- Do a sub-topic on human population growth and problems of over-crowding in many of the world's cities. Consider whether the world may have too many people, and what the impacts will be of future population increases.

# R.E.

- If you consider the children to be old enough, discuss the ethical aspects of population control – i.e. whether people should be limited in the number of children they can have because of the over-population of our planet.
- Discuss similarities and differences that occur amongst people from all over the world. Help children to appreciate that, whatever the colour of our skin, we are all human beings with the same basic needs. One of the key differences between people is their personal beliefs and faiths: use this as a basis for exploring some of the world's major religions.
- Tell the Old Testament story of how life began on Earth, and of how the world's first people came into being.

# MATHEMATICS

**Using and applying mathematics**
All activities below provide opportunities for using and applying mathematics.

**Number**
- Do 'people' sums. Prepare calculations for the children to solve based on numbers of people in families, in the school, etc., for example, counting family members in a family tree. [1a, 2a, 2b, 4a-d, 5b]
- Find out statistics relating to local and global population, for example, how many people there are in your school, village, town, country, and in the whole world. Whilst many statistics will be relatively meaningless in real terms, they will help develop an awareness of number and encourage children to realise that human population figures are BIG. [1a-f, 2a, 2b, 4a-d, 5b]
- Decide how to handle and interpret data collected in other areas of the project, for example, on journeys, work routines, homes. Maintain and use appropriate databases; construct and interpret statistical diagrams. [1e, 3e, 4c, 5b]

# ART

**Investigating and making**
- Make a huge colourful wall frieze on 'The Human Face', utilising pictures of people from all over the world cut from magazines or tourist brochures, or displaying children's own paintings. Annotate with writing describing similarities and differences between races and nations.
- Make paintings, portraits or collages of people in times gone by, paying particular attention to details such as hairstyles, clothing and backgrounds.

**Knowledge and understanding**
- Look at and talk about examples of the work of well-known artists on the theme of people/portraits. If possible, visit an art gallery for this purpose. Discuss how the artist portrays personality, personal appearance, moods and feelings, etc.

# CITIZENSHIP

- Discuss how every individual can take a positive and active role in the life of the local community, helping people in a community group to feel a sense of corporate identity and belonging. Look for ways in which citizenship feelings and actions can be developed in your own community.

# ENGLISH

**Speaking and listening**
- Investigate the differences that exist between tones of human voice: ask the children to listen carefully to each other, either 'live' or on recording tape. Talk about who has the deepest voice, the softest, the loudest, etc. [1a-d, 2a-b, 3a-b]
- Remind children that being able to speak is a major difference between humans and other animals; but not all people speak in the same way. Listen to people from around the world and discuss the great variety of languages we use. Obtain audio tapes for this purpose. [1a-d, 2a-b, 3a-b]
- Learn to speak some words of another language. [1c, 2b, 3a-b]

**Reading**
- Read stories, poems and rhymes about people (perhaps of differing characters, from other lands, behaving in certain ways, doing certain jobs, etc.) for the children to respond to; or provide a range of such material for the children to read themselves. [1a-d, 2a-c, 3]
- Set up a reading corner of non-fiction material on the theme of people, for the children to delve into and use for specific research purposes. [1b-c, 2a-b, 2d, 3]

**Writing**
- Suggest that the children produce a range of pieces of writing, for example, poems, stories, rhymes, factual

accounts, describing in real or imaginary terms people in various situations. Titles or themes might include 'People Who Help Us', 'People In Different Moods' (such as sadness, anger, temper, patience, concentration, fear), 'People From Distant Lands', 'People Who make Us Laugh', 'People In The Street', 'My Neighbours', 'The World's Nicest People', 'Why People Sometimes Annoy Me'. [1a-c, 2a-e, 3a-b]

● Write up coherently the results of observations of people in various situations, for example, of the observations of each other in the classroom, of people in the street. [1a-c, 2a-e, 3a-b]

● Ask the children to write symbols or isolated words to communicate their feelings about pictures of people with various expressions on their faces. [1a-c, 2a-e, 3a-b]

● Ask children to write a description (based on physical appearance, personality or both) of their friend or of another anonymous class member. Read aloud the results so that the rest of the class can try to guess the person being described. [1a-c, 2a-e, 3a-b]

● Write similar descriptions of well-known people such as TV personalities for the children to read out and identify. [1a-c, 2a-e, 3a-b]

# MUSIC

## Listening and appraising

● Listen to music composed and played by people from a variety of cultural backgrounds. Discuss how rhythms are used to achieve effects, and talk about differences and similarities that characterise pieces listened to. Help children to appreciate how certain musical styles and instruments characterise people from certain locations in the world.

## Blueprints links

**Art Key Stage 1:** complete chapter on my family and myself, copymasters 1, 6, 9; **Art Resource Bank:** complete chapter on people, copymasters 63–86; **Assemblies 5–8:** photocopiable assembly on people who help us; **Christmas Key Stage 1:** topic on caring; **Christmas Art and Craft:** mask making activities; **Distant Places:** activities about people in six different countries; **Early Years Songs and Rhymes:** many songs and rhymes on the topic; **Environmental Education Key Stage 1:** topic on work; **Geography Key Stage 1:** copymasters on jobs people do; **Health Education Key Stage 1:** many activities and copymasters on health and people; **History Key Stage 1:** huge bank of activities and copymasters on people then and now; **Infant Geography Resource Bank:** copymasters on people who work and help, 15, 25, 41–47; **Infant Teacher's Resource Bank:** copymasters 92–99; **Poetry Book:** section on families, copymasters 9–12, 47; **Religious Education Key Stage 1:** topic on friendship and many activities and copymasters throughout; **Writing Book:** copymaster 43, **Science Key Stage 1:** activities and copymasters; **Second Key Stage 1 Topics Book:** complete topic on people who help us, with copymasters.

# THE EARTH IN SPACE

## THE EARTH IN SPACE

## ENGLISH

- Observe local landscape and sky
- Read and tell space stories and poems
- Investigate planet Earth, the solar system and space exploration
- Talk about the Earth in Space
- Write stories and poems about space
- Label posters, pictures and writing used for display
- Read non-fiction reference material
- Produce factual writing, including results of scientific investigations

## R.E.

- Discuss the beginning of the Earth and theories about its creation
- Read or tell the Biblical version of the Creation

## HEALTH EDUCATION

- Draw attention to the dangers of the sun's rays
- Discuss thunderstorms and the need to take care

## GEOGRAPHY

- Investigate the local environment
- Keep weather records
- Learn name of local area
- Look at maps of local environment and Great Britain
- Look at globe and world maps
- Investigate soil, rocks and stones
- Learn about minerals

## ART

- Make a variety of pictures relating to Earth in space
- Make models of spacecraft
- Tie and dye material
- Create a class frieze of Earth and space
- Study pictures of Earth in space
- Establish a classroom 'art gallery'

## MUSIC

- Create 'space music' including 'signals'
- Learn songs relating to space
- Use 'space music' for movement and creative dance
- Listen to selected pieces of music by well-known composers

## MATHEMATICS

- Predict outcomes of scientific investigations
- Add, subtract, estimate numbers associated with space travel
- Measure models of rockets/space craft
- Investigate fractions in relation to models
- Learn how to use simple weather instruments
- Invent space signals
- Discuss shapes used in models
- Probability in relation to space
- Represent data pictorially and on a database

## HISTORY

- Learn about man's early attempts to fly
- Tell and/or read myths and legends about space
- Learn about the first journey into space and the first moon landings
- Investigate the current space programme(s)
- Visit a museum of science or transport

## P.E. (DANCE)

- Explore movement and dance using selected 'space' music

## DESIGN AND TECHNOLOGY

- Design, plan, make and evaluate model rockets or spacecraft
- Construct simple database for storage and retrieval of space data
- Represent data on graphs, pie-charts, etc.

## SCIENCE

- Investigate the Earth in space
- Observe and record weather
- Learn about the importance of weather to life on Earth
- Investigate weathering
- Learn about natural and human-made materials
- Plant and grow seeds
- Investigate soils
- Learn about magnets and gravity
- Observe the position of the sun in the sky
- Learn position of Earth within solar system
- Find out about weather on other planets

**IDEAS BANK**

General starting points: Suggestions for programmes of study of core and foundation subjects relating to topic, and links with cross-curricular themes and R.E.

**STARTING POINTS**

• Begin by talking about the sky. Take the children outdoors so that they can observe the sky and the views around them. Warn them beforehand not to look directly at the sun, and explain the reasons for this. Talk about what the children can see, then introduce concepts of the atmosphere and space. Allow time for daily discussions about this topic, as the children should have much to contribute.

• Show pictures, photographs, videos, books, etc. about planet Earth in space, and discuss them with the children.

• Encourage the children to bring in their own contributions to the topic – books, models, pictures and so on – and talk about them. Encourage all children to participate in discussions.

• Look at a globe and talk about the planet Earth itself. Discuss the proportions of land and water which make up our planet, point out oceans and continents, ask the children to locate Great Britain and various other countries.

• Arrange a visit to a museum to look at exhibits relating to space travel.

# ENGLISH ▶

**Speaking and listening**

• Talk about space and the planet Earth. Let children talk about their existing knowledge of Earth and the solar system, planets, space travel and so on. [1a-d, 2a-b, 3a-b]

• Read or tell relevant stories and poems about space and space travel to the children. Talk about them all with the class and encourage individual contributions. [1a-d, 2a-b, 3a-b]

**Reading**

• Discuss the contents of space stories and poems. Give children the opportunity to read a poem or part of a story aloud to the class. [1a, 1c, 1d, 2a, 2b, 2c, 3]

• Let the children work in groups to plan and write an adventure story in space. When the stories are completed, let the children read or tell them to the rest of the class. Write them up in an illustrated class anthology for other children to read. [1a-d, 2a-d, 3]

**Writing**

• Write and illustrate imaginative stories/poems about space travel and the planets. Include dramatic accounts of a rocket launch, docking in space, or perhaps meeting an alien from outer space. [1a-c, 2a-e, 3a-b]

• Using secondary source material, help the children to produce factual writing about the Earth and space. [1a-c, 2a-e, 3a-b]

• Make informative labels for relevant classroom displays of writing and/or art work on the theme of space. [1a-c, 2a-e, 3a-b]

• Record details of science experiments. [1a-c, 2a-e, 3a-b]

# SCIENCE ▶

**Experimental and investigative science**

All activities below provide opportunities for experimental and investigative science.

• Look at appropriate space pictures/books/videotapes and other secondary source materials on the subject and encourage children to talk about them. Discuss Earth and its position in the solar system; talk about the sun and its importance to Earth. Observe weather, clouds, the position of the sun in the sky, and so on. [1a-d, 2a, 2b, 3a, 4a-b, 5a-b]

• Observe and record weather over a set period of time, and discuss your findings. Talk about our existing knowledge of weather on other planets in the solar system. [2b]

**Life processes and living things**

• Discuss weather (sunshine, rain and so on) and its importance to life on Earth. [1a-b, 2b, 3a-c, 5a-b]

• Organise an experiment to grow plants and test their need for water and light. Let children record details of plant growth throughout the experiment. Use correct names for parts of plants. [1a, 3a-c]

**Materials and their properties**

• Investigate different types of soil, such as clay, sand, loam, etc. Ask children to discover which soil is the most porous, the heaviest, etc. Record details of these experiments in appropriate ways. [1a-e, 2b]

• Discuss weathering and some of its causes. Talk about the weathering of buildings as well as that of rocks, cliffs, stones, etc. [1a-e, 2b]

• Consider what materials are used in school buildings and, for example, whether they are natural or human-made. Walk round the outside of the school (or part of it) with the children, and look for evidence of weathering – on woodwork, metal supports, brickwork, etc. [1a-e, 2b]

### Physical processes
- Investigate magnets. Introduce the concept of gravity. Discuss space rockets and the force needed to enable them to leave the gravitational pull of our Earth. If possible, let the children watch videotape recordings of rocket launching and man 'walking' on the moon. Discuss/compare moon gravity with that on Earth. Talk about weightlessness in space. [2a-d]
- With the aid of books and charts, study the position of the sun in the sky and its apparent movement throughout the day, and discuss it. [3a, 3b]
- Use secondary source material to look at the position of the Earth in relation to other planets and the sun. Let the children discuss their findings. [3a, 3b]
- Discuss the moon and its relation to the Earth. If possible, use books, film or videotape to illustrate the movement of the planets round the sun, and that of the moon around the Earth. [3a, 3b]

# MATHEMATICS ▶

### Using and applying mathematics
All activities below provide opportunities for using and applying mathematics.
- Encourage children to select the appropriate materials and mathematics as required when testing rockets/spaceships and/or measuring plant growth, weighing soil etc. [1a, 2a-d, 3a, 3b]
- Let children predict the outcomes of tests and discuss all work both as a class and individually. [1a-b, 2a-d, 3c, 4a, 4b]

### Number
- Discuss the various numbers used in space exploration, for example, countdown to zero and 'millions' when thinking about distances of the sun, moon and other planets from Earth, and from each other. Measure how long it takes to count to 10/20/100. Display numbers where all can see them. Is there time to count to 1000/10,000 before play/dinner, etc.? Practise counting as appropriate, for example, 1,2,3 ... or 10, 9, 8 ... etc. [1a-f, 1a, 1b, 3c, 5b]
- Discuss fractions – half, quarter, third – linked to the jettisoning of rocket sections during flight. Let the children make two-dimensional rockets using rectangles/triangles, colouring one half of the body (the rectangle) in, say, blue and the other half in red. [1a, 1c, 1e, 2c]
- Let children invent signals (patterns) from outer space and show these as repeat patterns on squared paper. [1a, 3a]
- Construct graphs, diagrams and/or charts to record weather information. [1e, 5b]
- Sort space models made by the children into sets (see Design and technology activities). [5a]

- Investigate probability, for example, it is certain/uncertain that this rocket will move along the ground if pushed, but impossible for it to fly up into space. [5b]
- Construct graphs, diagrams and/or charts to show which rockets travel furthest/fastest along the ground, which planet most children would like to visit, and so on. [1e, 5b]
- Design a simple data collection sheet for specified information, for example, the colours of planets, their distance from the Earth, their temperatures, or weather records for one or more weeks. Access this information using simple databases, giving children practice in selecting and retrieving information. [1f, 5b]

### Shape, space and measures
- Ask the children to estimate how long it would take to count to a given number (see number countdown), and then as a class, test these predictions. [1c, 4a-b]
- Measure the length and weight of model rockets. Test them for speed of movement. Do children consider length/weight relevant to performance? [1a, 1c, 4a-b]
- Show the children simple instruments for measuring temperature, rainfall, wind speed, etc., and let them all have plenty of practice in using them as they begin to keep weather records.[4a-b]
- Let the children compare and order their rockets without measuring. [1a, 1c, 4a]
- Discuss models made by the children, and talk about the shapes used in making real rockets/spacecraft. What shapes have been used? [1a, 2a-c]
- Use mathematical terms to describe common two-dimensional shapes and three-dimensional objects used when making models. [2a-c]

# DESIGN AND TECHNOLOGY ▶

### Design and technology capability
- Discuss the possibility of making individual/class rockets, spaceships, etc. Investigate the realities of the children's ideas and/or proposals. [1a-c, 2a-c]

### Designing skills
- Talk about, plan and design individual or class three-dimensional space models. [1a-f]

### Skills and knowledge and understanding
- Help the children to work individually or in small groups to finalise plans/designs and make models, using appropriate materials and tools. Be aware of safety issues at all times. [1a, 1b, 1c, 1d, 1e, 5a-g]
- Let all the children evaluate the results of their model making with both teacher and their peers in the class. [4f]

## Information technology

● Construct simple data collection sheet(s) to show selected details about the Earth and other planets/the results of individual rocket testing/weather records and so on. Give children practice in entering, amending and retrieving this information. [1b, 1c, 2b, 2c, 3a, 3b]

● Discuss other methods of recording statistical information, such as graphs, pie charts, pictograms, etc. [1a, 2a]

# ART ▶

## Investigating and making

● Using varied materials and techniques (such as collage, paint, tie and dye, glitter, printing, etc.) let children produce imaginary representations of the Earth in space. Encourage children to discuss their completed work.

● Use dark blue or black dye on white material to produce a backcloth for a space design. Show children how to prepare the material for tie and dye work. When it has been dyed and ironed, let the children use it for sewing a space picture using the white parts still remaining as an imaginary background for stars, comets, space ships and so on. Complete the pictures with a little glitter and/or some sequins.

● Collect models of space craft/rockets and let children design and make their own.

● Design a class frieze, for example, 'The Planets In Space' (place the planets in their correct order from the sun), 'Journey To The Stars', and so on.

## Knowledge and understanding

● Look at appropriate pictures relating to the topic, including if possible some historical ones. How did the more visionary artists of the past represent the possibilities of space travel? Discuss these pictures, observing similarities and differences between imaginary space craft and the modern day reality. If actual pictures are difficult to obtain, consider showing the children extracts from old films such as the Flash Gordon serials of the 1930s (which are occasionally revived on television), 'War Of The Worlds', and more recent productions such as '2001: A Space Odyssey', the 'Star Wars' and/or 'Star Trek' series. Ask the children to observe and comment upon the space designs and effects they see. How many are realistic, and how many are pure fantasy? (Remember to check the copyright position before showing commercial video-tapes in school.)

● Relate these pictures to the children's own work.

● Discuss themes and any pictures creating atmosphere/mood.

# GEOGRAPHY ▶

## Geographical skills and places

● Study the local environment around the school or in a local park. Look at soil, rocks and stones. Collect 'interesting' stones, and notice any effects of weathering on them. Encourage children to bring in any stones or rocks of their own, but stress that they must be interesting or different in some way. Help a class collection by introducing some semi-precious stones, for example, a small piece of rose quartz, or dragon's eye, or amethyst, and so on. Collect stones from other countries and make a class display of them. [1a-c, 2, 3a-f]

● Record local weather conditions over a period of time. [1a, 2, 3e, 3f, 4, 5c]

● Discuss the local area and where children live. Help them to name their village/town/city and the country in which they live. Pinpoint their home town on a map of the British Isles. If some children in the class have come to the school from elsewhere (other towns, cities or even countries) then perhaps a similar activity could be carried out in order to establish their origins: record the results on a globe or maps of the world, if appropriate. [1a-c, 2, 3a, 3b, 3e, 3f, 4]

● Look at a globe and world maps. Locate the British Isles and 'discover' other well-known countries, for example, those currently in the news for some reason or those suggested by the children. Help the children to become accustomed to viewing the Earth as shown by a globe. Point out the angle at which the globe is set and relate this to the Earth in space. [1c, 3e]

● Let the children investigate rocks/stones brought in for display. Discuss them and consult relevant books, pictures, etc. in order to discover as much about these exhibits as possible. [1a-c, 2, 3a, 3b, 3e, 3f]

● Examine stones brought in from the seashore and any others worn smooth/away by water/wind, etc. Discuss this process with the children. [1a-c, 2, 3a, 3b, 3e, 3f]

● Let the children look at pictures from other parts of the world, for example, rock formations showing weathering or worn away by water courses, etc. Discuss effects of weather in relation to other climates. [1c, 2, 3e, 3f]

● Talk about some of the valuable materials obtained from the Earth, such as coal, minerals, chalk, etc. [1c, 2, 3e, 3f, 4, 5a, 5b]

# HISTORY

**Areas of study (Key Elements 1-5)**
- Stimulate class discussions about the time before people could travel into space – and about our efforts to fly. If possible, show appropriate films or videotapes of early flying machines as well as looking at books and pictures. [1a-b, 2, 3]
- Tell the children some myths/fantasies about space (the man in the moon, the moon is made of green cheese, the stars are people who used to live on Earth, etc.) and ask if the children are aware of others. Tell them stories about the stars from Greek mythology. Discuss fact and fiction with regard to outer space. [1a-b, 2, 3]
- Talk about the first journey into space, and the main stages of progression in space exploration to date. Discuss man's moon landings, watch any relevant films or videotapes of these events; consider the space probe to Mars, with its problems of camera failure, etc. [2, 3]
- Visit a museum of science or transport in your area, if this is possible. [2, 3]
- Study as much visual evidence of space flight as possible – pictures, photographs, films, videotapes, etc. – and discuss each item with the children. [2, 3]

# MUSIC

**Performing and composing**
- Let the children create imaginative sounds from outer space, planet echoes, etc., and include their mathematical 'space signals' patterns. Play these sounds on instruments of their own choice.
- Learn songs relating to the topics of outer space and flight. The latter suggests a number of different songs, both old and new (such as 'Up, Up And Away', 'Me And Jane In A Plane', 'Those Magnificent Men In Their Flying Machines').
- Let children compose their own space music, either in small groups or individually, on themes such as star music, spaceship music and so on. After a suitable rehearsal period, record these pieces and play them to others.

**Listening and appraising**
- Let the children listen to selected passages of music with interplanetary or astrological connections, such as Holst's 'Planets Suite', Manuel de Falla's 'Ritual Fire Dance' (the sun), and so on.
- Use space music for movement and creative dance.
- Talk about the different kinds of chosen music and compare it with everyday sounds.

# P.E.

**Dance**
- Let the children explore movement and dance by working with appropriate space music. Suggest children work in groups to create in dance an imaginary space story. Let each group show its dance to the others.

# R.E.

- Talk about various theories of how the world began, for example, the scientific theory and various religious beliefs. Tell the Biblical version of the Creation.

# HEALTH EDUCATION

- During class discussions, talk about the danger of (i) looking directly into the sun, (ii) staying out in the sun too long without adequate protection (sunstroke, tanning the skin), and (iii) sheltering under trees in a thunderstorm.

**Blueprints links**
**Early Years Songs and Rhymes:** pages 5, 9; **Infant Teacher's Resource Bank:** copymasters 138 (picture of the earth in space), 139; **Poetry Book:** section on space, copymasters 57–60; **Religious Education Key Stage 1:** copymaster 80; **Science Key Stage 1:** activities in **Physical processes:** copymasters 87–89; **Seasonal Activities:** summer 2, Winter 2; **Writing 5–8:** copymasters 42–45.

# CLIMATE

**CLIMATE**

## ENGLISH

- Study local weather
- Read and tell weather stories and poems
- Discuss which weather conditions are most popular
- Investigate weather in other areas of the globe
- Write imaginary weather stories/poems
- Label classroom display(s)
- Write factual accounts about different climatic zones
- Record details of scientific investigations
- Write factual accounts of school visit(s)

## GEOGRAPHY

- Study and record weather
- Learn about this country's climate
- Investigate the globe in relation to climatic zones
- Study in detail 2 or 3 different climates, including people and natural resources

## ART

- Make a wide range of weather pictures
- Use clay to model animals from specific climatic zones
- Arrange display of animals in their zones when models are finished
- Make a working weather vane or windmill
- Design a weather wall frieze
- Study pictures, books, etc. relating to climatic zones
- List the main differences of each zone
- Look at relevant paintings and discuss these

## MUSIC

- Explore musical interpretation of weather by using patterns/instruments
- Learn a selection of weather songs
- Create movement and dance associated with weather
- Listen to selected pieces of music by well-known composers

## MATHEMATICS

- Learn how to use simple weather instruments
- Record weather measurements
- Use a maximum/minimum thermometer
- Learn the 8 points of a compass
- Study wind speed
- Reproduce data pictorially and on a database
- Discuss probability in relation to weather

## HISTORY

- Investigate changes in all climatic zones
- Study pictures, books, etc. illustrating life in each climatic zone
- Discuss the difference between fact and fiction
- Look at pictures for evidence of how people live or lived
- Tell stories of well-known people associated with each climatic zone, e.g. Scott and the Antarctic

## P.E. (DANCE)

- Use selected music to create weather dances

## DESIGN AND TECHNOLOGY

- Discuss making class instruments to measure weather
- Design, plan, make and evaluate the weather instruments
- Construct simple database for storage and retrieval of weather records

## SCIENCE

- Investigate other specified world climates
- Undertake class experiments growing seeds/plants
- Predict outcome of tests
- Study conditions necessary for survival of plants, animals and humans
- Investigate temperatures
- Discuss wind force
- Visit a botanical garden, or similar

## IDEAS BANK

General starting points: Suggestions for programmes of study of core and foundation subjects relating to topic, and links with cross-curricular themes and R.E.

## STARTING POINTS

- With the class, observe and discuss local weather conditions over a period of days.
- Look at pictures, books, videotape recordings etc showing desert lands, polar lands, rain forests, storms and so on. Discuss these over a period of time.
- Look at a globe and show children the position of Great Britain in relation to the Poles and the Equator. Talk about broad bands of different climatic conditions in relation to the shape/angle of Earth in space and the rays of the sun. Discuss and show the Earth's movement in relation to the sun. Use the children themselves to represent the sun, earth, moon and planets: show them how to move as if they were in space. Let the other children watch and then take turns themselves.
- Show children simple instruments for measuring the weather. Introduce them one at a time: let children practise reading and recording the temperature, and using the other equipment.
- If possible, arrange a visit to a botanical garden where children can experience rain forest temperatures and conditions, observe and record cacti growing in simulated desert conditions, etc. You may prefer to do this when the topic is under way.

# ENGLISH ▶

### Speaking and listening

- Talk about weather in general. Let children discuss their favourite kind of weather, or the type of weather they dislike most. Encourage them to give reasons for their likes and dislikes. [1a-d, 2a-b, 3a-b]
- Discuss other weather conditions in deserts, polar lands, rain forests and how they differ from our own. [1a-d, 2a-b, 3a-b]
- Let the children work in small groups to plan an imaginary story involving weather. Help them with the beginning of the story, if necessary. When they are ready, ask the children to tell their stories to each other. [1a-d, 2a-b, 3a-b]
- Tell or read weather poems and stories to children and discuss them afterwards. [1a-d, 2a-b, 3a-b]

### Reading

- Talk about the content and structure of some of the weather poems and stories. Let children participate in the reading aloud. [1a, 1c, 1d, 2a, 2b, 2c, 3]

- Work with children to produce a beginning for a weather story, ask them to predict what might happen next and how the story will end. Let them write and/or draw their own middle and/or end and then read or tell their story to the rest of the class. [1a, 1c, 1d, 2a, 2b, 2c, 3]

### Writing

- Let children write imaginary stories involving weather, for example, 'Lost In The Snow', 'When The Rain Wouldn't Stop', 'How I Lost My Kite', 'Pink Snow', and so on. [1a-c, 2a-e, 3a-b]
- Make labels and write information about a class display of models and items brought in by children. [1a-c, 2a-e, 3a-b]
- Record the details of any science experiments on weather. [1a-c, 2a-e, 3a-b]
- Write factual accounts about different climates and their peoples. [1a-c, 2a-e, 3a-b]
- Write factual account(s) of any school visit to observe aspects of the weather. [1a-c, 2a-e, 3a-b]

# SCIENCE ▶

### Experimental and investigative science

All activities below provide opportunities for experimental and investigative science.

- Consider differences in the climates being studied, and let children talk about their own weather experiences. [1a, 1b, 1c, 2a, 2b, 3a, 4a-b]

### Life processes and living things

- Suggest that the children experiment with plants and try to grow them in the 'wrong' climatic conditions for a short period of time – for example, put a cactus outside to grow, grow one indoors and water daily; grow a tropical plant in dry conditions, indoor/outdoor; put a plant in the school fridge, and so on. Record what happens. [1a, 3a-c, 4b, 5a-b]

(NOTE: If possible, remove these plants from their 'wrong' growing conditions before they die!)

- Talk about the conditions needed for plants, animals and humans to survive. Discuss how living things have adapted to different climates. [1a, 3a-c, 4b, 5a-b]

### Physical processes

- Draw attention to heat and cold in relation to everyday temperatures and weather conditions, for example, in terms of wind force. [2a-d, 3a-b]
- When discussing wind speed talk about direction and how to use a weather vane. [2a-d]

# MATHEMATICS

**Using and applying mathematics**
All activities below provide opportunities for using and applying mathematics.

**Shape, space and measures**
- Let the children select appropriate materials and mathematics for recording and measuring the weather. [1c, 4b]
- Discuss individually and/or as a class any problems encountered. [1c, 4b]
- Show the children how to use a thermometer correctly, preferably an indoor/outdoor one so that difference in temperature can be discussed. Let children have daily practice in reading/recording temperature, and in keeping their own weather diaries over a period of time so that temperature and general weather conditions can be recorded daily. [1a, 1c, 4b]

- Learn to use a maximum and minimum thermometer. [1a, 1c, 4b]

**Number**
- Let the children work individually or in small groups to design graphs and other diagrams for recording aspects of the weather. Discuss these recording methods and let children use them. Ask the children to use their records to extract specific information – for example, what was the coldest day? How many rainy days have we had this month? [1a, 1c, 1e, 1f, 5b]
- Talk about probability in relation to weather – for example, is it certain that it will rain tonight? Is there a good chance that we shall have snow today? [5b]

# DESIGN AND TECHNOLOGY

**Design and technology capability**
- Talk about the local climate, the children's own weather records and available instruments for measuring wind, rainfall, temperature, etc. [1a-c, 2a-c]
- Discuss making class instruments, whether it is possible to make rain gauges, weather vanes and so on. [1a-c, 2a-c]

**Designing skills**
- Let the children decide what kind of weather measurement instruments they would like to design. (Some guidance may be necessary if ideas are too ambitious!) Discuss possibilities and let children make drawings and/or plans where appropriate. [3a-f]

**Making skills and knowledge and understanding**
- Let the children select appropriate materials from as wide a range as possible, and with discussion and help where required, let them make their chosen piece of apparatus. [4a, 4b, 4c, 4d, 4e, 5a-g]
- Let the children test and/or demonstrate their finished instruments and evaluate performance. [4f]

**Information technology**
- Structure a simple database to record weather details. Help children to input, select, sort and retrieve information as required. [1a-c, 2b, 2c, 3a, 3b]

# ART

**Investigating and making**
- Encourage the children to use as wide a range of materials and techniques as possible to make representations of the weather.
- Let the children create pictures linked with the overall climate of (a) Great Britain, (b) desert lands, (c) polar lands, and (d) rain forests. Use as many different and appropriate techniques as possible, such as wool/string collage, differently textured paper and/or material, sponge paint, splatter paint, and so on.
- Discuss animal life in different climates. Divide the class into four groups and let children make individual clay animals from specific climatic zones. Paint these models in realistic colours and arrange a display for

each zone. Let the children study pictures to help with accuracy of modelling.
- Look at pictures and then plan/design either a working weather vane or a rain gauge.
- Design a wall frieze or four large wall pictures depicting each of the climatic zones listed above. Ensure that all children contribute to this activity in some way. Discuss the work with them and allow them to change their original plan or design if necessary. Evaluate the work with the whole class.

**Knowledge and understanding**
- Encourage the children to bring in relevant pictures and/or photographs and discuss differences

between the two in terms of accurate portrayal of weather/climatic conditions.

- Look at other pictures relevant to the topic and discuss them. Try to obtain prints of paintings by well known artists and encourage children to look at techniques, detail, mood and so on.

# GEOGRAPHY

**Geographical skills and places**

- Discuss and record weather conditions over a period of time. [1a-c, 2, 3a, 3b, 3c, 3e, 3f]
- Help the children to learn the eight points of a compass, and relate these to such things as wind direction. [2, 3c]
- Compare weather conditions in this country with other world climates studied. [1a-c, 2, 3a, 3e, 3f, 4, 5c]
- Look at the globe in relation to climatic zones. Discuss briefly the reasons for changes in climates, for example, the angle of the Earth in space and its movement around the sun. [1c, 2, 3e, 3f]

**Geographical skills and thematic study**

- Discuss in detail contrasting climates. Study various climatic zones such as polar lands or tropical places in detail, looking at weather conditions, flora and fauna, and people. Encourage children to bring in books, pictures and articles from the relevant zones. Display these in the appropriate area of the classroom. [1c, 2, 3e, 3f, 6a-c]
- Discuss the lives of people living in climates different from our own, together with the similarities and differences of such lifestyles. [1a-c, 2, 3a, 3b, 3e, 3f, 4, 5c, 6a-c]
- Look at natural resources in the areas being studied and relate them, if possible, to the appropriate climatic conditions. [1a-c, 2, 3a, 3b, 3e, 3f, 4, 5c, 6a-c]

# HISTORY

**Areas of study (Key Elements 1-5)**

- When investigating each climatic zone discuss with the children how life has changed for people living there. Why? How? (Mention, for example, that the Inuit people no longer commonly live in igloos.) [1a-b, 2, 3]
- Look at pictures of people in different climatic zones and talk about how they used to live and how they live today. Introduce the concept of fact as opposed to a

point of view, and make children aware that they are talking about real people, not fictional characters. [1a-b, 2, 3]

- Examine available evidence such as pictures, photographs of people who lived in different climatic zones in the past, also photographs and other pictorial evidence of how they live today. Encourage children to look closely at these and extract as much information as possible. [1a-b, 2, 3]

# MUSIC

**Performing and composing**

- Discuss different aspects of weather in relation to sounds and rhythm patterns. Reproduce these patterns using various instruments; record them visually and let children practise playing each other's rhythms.
- Learn some songs about the weather, the animals in various climatic zones and so on. Let the children experiment with instruments, to accompany singers in some songs.
- Let the children work in small groups to compose weather music representing, for example, sunshine, rain, storm decreasing in intensity to sunshine once again. Record these compositions and

play them for the other children to discuss and exchange ideas.

**Listening and appraising**

- Let the children listen to some traditional music from the British Isles, together with passages of music from other lands included in the topic. Discuss this music, its similarities and differences; talk about rhythm, pitch, dynamics etc., and the instruments used. Can the children name any of these instruments?
- Let the children respond to selected music in movement and dance.

# P.E.

**Dance**
- Use selected appropriate music for movement and creative dance. Discuss with the children the moods and images projected through the music.

**Blueprints links**
**Art Resource Bank:** copymasters 61–2; **Assemblies 5–8:** photocopiable assemblies on the seasons; **Distant Places:** activities and information about climate in different parts of the world; **Early Years Songs and Rhymes:** many songs and rhymes on the weather; **Environmental Education Key Stage 1:** topic on weather; **Geography Key Stage 1:** 101–10; **Infant Geography Resource Bank:** section on weather and climate, copymasters 91–102; **Infant Teacher's Resource Bank:** copymasters 47–50 (seasons); **Poetry Book:** sections on wind and storm, copymasters 29–32, and elements, copymasters 37–40; **Religious Eductaion Key Stage 1:** copymasters 109–111; **Writing book;** copymasters 21, 57, 64, 66, 69, 70, 80, 92; **Seasonal Activities:** many activities on climate.

# RAIN

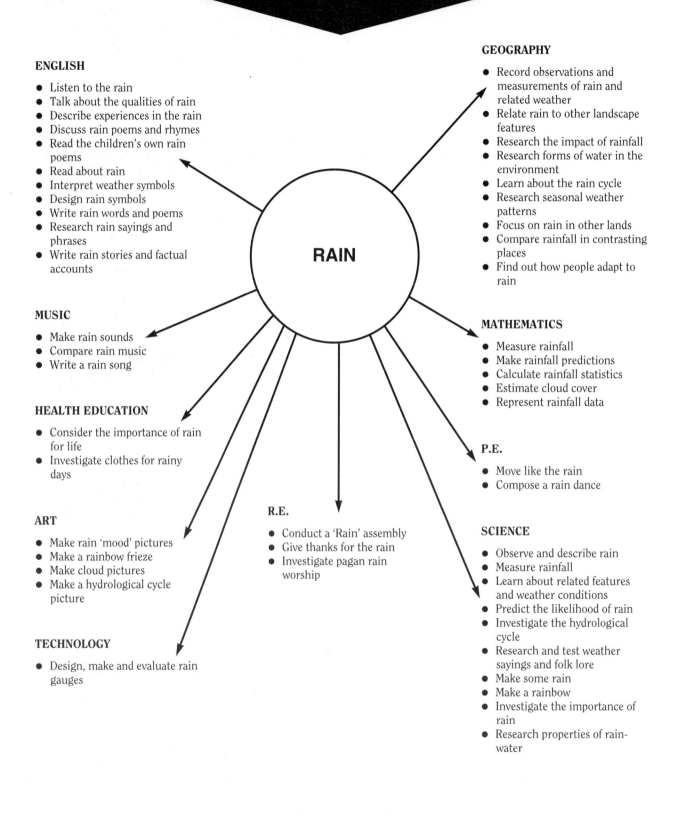

## ENGLISH

- Listen to the rain
- Talk about the qualities of rain
- Describe experiences in the rain
- Discuss rain poems and rhymes
- Read the children's own rain poems
- Read about rain
- Interpret weather symbols
- Design rain symbols
- Write rain words and poems
- Research rain sayings and phrases
- Write rain stories and factual accounts

## MUSIC

- Make rain sounds
- Compare rain music
- Write a rain song

## HEALTH EDUCATION

- Consider the importance of rain for life
- Investigate clothes for rainy days

## ART

- Make rain 'mood' pictures
- Make a rainbow frieze
- Make cloud pictures
- Make a hydrological cycle picture

## TECHNOLOGY

- Design, make and evaluate rain gauges

## R.E.

- Conduct a 'Rain' assembly
- Give thanks for the rain
- Investigate pagan rain worship

## GEOGRAPHY

- Record observations and measurements of rain and related weather
- Relate rain to other landscape features
- Research the impact of rainfall
- Research forms of water in the environment
- Learn about the rain cycle
- Research seasonal weather patterns
- Focus on rain in other lands
- Compare rainfall in contrasting places
- Find out how people adapt to rain

## MATHEMATICS

- Measure rainfall
- Make rainfall predictions
- Calculate rainfall statistics
- Estimate cloud cover
- Represent rainfall data

## P.E.

- Move like the rain
- Compose a rain dance

## SCIENCE

- Observe and describe rain
- Measure rainfall
- Learn about related features and weather conditions
- Predict the likelihood of rain
- Investigate the hydrological cycle
- Research and test weather sayings and folk lore
- Make some rain
- Make a rainbow
- Investigate the importance of rain
- Research properties of rain-water

**IDEAS BANK**

General starting points: Suggestions for programmes of study of core and foundation subjects relating to topic, and links with cross-curricular themes and R.E.

**STARTING POINTS**

● Begin the topic on a rainy day – go out for a walk in the rain (if the children have weatherproof clothing) or watch and listen to it through the window.

● Make a collection of pictures/photographs of rainy scenes, including related phenomena such as thunderstorms and rainbows.

● Make some rain in the classroom through practical science activities.

● Read poems and rhymes about rain and rainy days.

# ENGLISH ▶

**Speaking and listening**

● Listen to the rain – either outdoors or pattering onto a roof or window. Talk about the sound it makes. [1a-d, 2a-b, 3a-b]

● Talk about and make lists of 'rain words' which describe its feel, appearance, sounds, etc. Let the children articulate words they have made up (sploshy, splushy, etc.) as well as familiar words. [1a-d, 2a-b, 3a-b]

● Ask the children to describe experiences they have had of being in the rain – perhaps walking or driving through a torrential storm – and to tell the listeners how they felt. [1a-d, 2a-b, 3a-b]

● Discuss poems and rhymes which have rain or related topics as their themes. [1a-d, 2a-b, 3a-b]

● Let the children read out loud their own stories, real or imaginary, about rain and related topics, for discussion and questioning by other members of the class. [1a-d, 2a-b, 3a-b]

**Reading**

● Set up a display of non-fiction and fiction material about rain and related topics (clouds, weather, thunder, floods, storms, rainbows, etc.) for the children to consult for pleasure and guided research purposes. [1a-d, 2a-d, 3]

● Organise times for reading aloud and discussion of stories, rhymes and poems about rain, paying close attention to expression of appropriate mood and feeling. [1a, 1c, 1d, 2a, 2b, 2c, 3]

● Read and interpret weather symbols – on TV maps and your own classroom displays. [1a, b, c, 2a, d]

**Writing**

● Design pictures, symbols or simple words to represent rain and related weather conditions. Use these on classroom weather recording charts. [1a-c, 2a-e, 3]

● Write lists of words which describe rain and associated conditions and phenomena. [1a-c, 2a-e, 3b]

● Use your 'rain words' as the basis for writing expressive, descriptive poems, and factual accounts about the subject. [1a-c, 2a-e, 3a-b]

● Research, write out and illustrate sayings and proverbs about rain, such as 'raining cats and dogs', 'raining buckets' etc. [1a-c, 2a-e, 3a-b]

● Write factual or imaginative stories about rainy or storm conditions, suggesting titles if appropriate – 'The Flood', 'At The End Of The Rainbow', 'Storm At Sea', 'The Day The Rain Was Pink', 'Caught In The Storm', and so on. [1a-c, 2a-e, 3a-b]

● Write carefully researched accounts about rain – its formation, significance, benefits and problems (relate to geography and science activities). [1a-c, 2a-e, 3a-b]

# SCIENCE ▶

**Experimental and investigative science**

All activities below provide opportunities for experimental and investigative science.

● Observe rainfall and describe carefully its qualities, and impacts upon where it falls. [1a-c, 2a-c, 3a-f]

● Measure rainfall, designing and utilising appropriate instruments. [1a-c, 2a-c, 3a-f]

● Link the falling of rain to related weather and atmospheric conditions, and hence learn why rain falls, and what conditions are necessary in order for this to happen. [1a-c, 2a-c, 3a-f]

● Investigate the hydrological cycle (link with geography activities). [1a-c, 2a-c, 3a-f]

● Study various cloud types, and make predictions about ensuing weather, and the likelihood of rainfall. Find out whether your amateur forecasting is accurate. [1a-c, 2a-c, 3a-f]

● Do further sub-topics and further investigations about related themes and phenomena including thunder and thunderstorms, hurricanes, sleet, snow, clouds, rainbows and hail. Find out about the weather conditions necessary for these phenomena to occur. Observe, make predictions about and measure as many of these as possible. [1a-c, 2a-c, 3a-f]

● Research weather sayings and folklore about rain, for example, the story of St. Swithin's Day. If possible, test some of your discoveries, paying attention to the need for fair testing. [1a-c, 2a-c, 3a-f]

- Make some 'rain' in the classroom; consult books on practical science for suggestions on creating condensation indoors. [1a-c, 2a-c, 3a-f]
- Make a 'rainbow' on a white wall in the classroom by shining sunlight onto a mirror in water. [1a-c, 2a-c, 3a-f]

### Life processes and living things
- Appreciate that rainfall is essential for life on Earth. The water it supplies is necessary for all forms of animal, plant and human life. [1a-b, 2b, 2c, 3a, 5a-b]

### Materials and their properties
- Undertake tests to see if rainwater 'behaves' in the same ways as tap water and perhaps ocean water: freeze it, boil it, etc. Research the differences between rainwater, salt water and tap water. [1a-e, 2b]

# MATHEMATICS ▶

### Using and applying mathematics
All activities below provide opportunities for using and applying mathematics.
- Discuss the appropriate mathematics and materials needed for measuring rainfall over a period of time and utilise these. [1a-b, 2a-d, 3a-d, 4a-c]
- Make predictions about the mathematics of rainfall measurements. Use appropriate mathematics to test these and solve related problems. [1a-b, 2a-d, 3a-d, 4a-c]

### Number
- Add rainfall measurements over a period of time to calculate weekly fall, monthly fall, etc. [1a, 1e, 1f, 2a, 2b, 3c, 3e]
- Estimate sky cloud cover – traditionally done by estimating how many eighths of the sky are covered with cloud. Begin by estimating more or less than half ... quarter, etc. [1a, 1c, 1e, 1f, 2c, 4a, 5b]
- Interpret data collected on the amount of rainfall: work out the rainiest day, the least rainy day, put days in rank order, etc. [1e, 1f, 5a-b]
- Represent data on appropriate graphs and diagrams, also on a database. [1e, 1f, 5a-b]
- Draw graphs and diagrams and use databases to show comparisons in rainfall statistics in local and distant places (relate to geography activities). [1e, 1f, 5a-b]

# GEOGRAPHY ▶

### Geographical skills and places
- Record observations and measurement of rainfall over a period of time. [1a-c, 2]
- Make more detailed observations, measurements and recordings of aspects of the weather, helping children to understand the links, if any, between rainfall and other features such as clouds, wind, rainbow, temperature, etc. [1a-c, 2, 3a, 3e, 3f]
- Observe rain falling on to the ground. Discuss where it goes. Link with identification and understanding of other landscape features such as lakes, streams, rivers, oceans. [1a-c, 2, 3a, 3b, 3c, 3e, 3f]
- Discuss and investigate all of the forms in which water occurs in the environment, for example, in various states (water vapour, liquid rain, frozen as sleet and snow) and as various landscape features – lakes, oceans, rivers, ponds, etc. [1a-c, 2, 3a, 3b, 3c, 3e, 3f, 4, 5a-d]
- Closely observe rainwater falling on the ground – on both paved surfaces and open space. Discuss and investigate what happens to it. Link with further work on drainage systems, soil erosion, flooding, etc. [1a-c, 2, 3a, 3b, 3c, 3e, 3f]
- Help children to appreciate that rainfall is part of a cycle of natural events involving clouds, the oceans, the land, evaporation and condensation. Write about and illustrate 'The Rain Cycle'. [1a-c, 2, 3e, 3d, 5b, 5c]
- As a result of personal experiences, weather observations and further reading, recognise seasonal weather patterns. Discuss in which season it is likely that we may have most rain, sleet, snow, thunderstorms, etc. [1a-e, 2, 3e, 3f]
- Undertake a sub-topic on rain in different parts of the world, perhaps focusing on features such as tropical rain forests, monsoon areas, lands with too little rain. [1c, 2, 3e, 3f, 4, 5a-d]
- Obtain rainfall statistics for various months of the year from a range of distant lands. Compare and contrast them. [2, 3e, 3f, 5a-d]
- Research how people who live in lands with a great deal of rain adapt to such wet conditions, for example, by building houses on stilts. [1c, 2, 3e, 3f, 4, 5a-d]

# HEALTH EDUCATION

**Health education**
- Reinforce an understanding of the importance of rain for maintaining life in all its forms (link with science activities). Research how our own bodies are kept alive by rain, through a study of how we obtain our drinking water.

- Talk about clothes that are suitable for rainy weather, and why people try to keep themselves dry as far as possible. Do this in a balanced way, pointing out that sometimes it may be fun to get wet in the rain, especially on a warm summer's day.

# ART

**Investigating and making**
- Create paintings and collages of rainy days, thunderstorms and cloudy conditions, paying particular attention to colour and 'mood'.
- Make a huge collage rainbow to span the classroom wall over a frieze board. Add a collage sun above it. Cut raindrops from foil or film and attach them to the frieze board around pieces of writing on the topic.

- Make cloud pictures. Paint clouds or print them, paying attention to real cloud types and formations – encourage the children to think about a range of shades of the colours white and grey. Distinguish, for example, between fair weather clouds and heavy, dark, cumulo-nimbus thunder clouds.
- Make a large wall picture of the hydrological (rain) cycle.

# MUSIC

**Performing and composing**
- Discuss the sounds made by rain – pitter-patter, splash, etc. Create these sounds on a range of instruments. Compose your own rain music!
- Write words about the rain to accompany your rain sounds, creating a rain song.

**Listening and appraising**
- Listen to as many songs or pieces of music about rain, its features and its consequences as possible, including folk songs, classical music and so on.

# P.E.

**Dance**
- Move like the rain. Compose your own rain dance involving various forms of rain and movement – for example, a light shower, a fierce thunderstorm, a hurri-

cane, a strong steady downpour. Accompany with your own rain music or sound effects of rain obtainable on recordings from your local library.

# DESIGN AND TECHNOLOGY

**Design and technology capability**
- Talk about how to measure rainfall and the need for appropriate instruments to do this. [1a-c, 2a-c]

**Designing skills**
- Design one or more rain gauges. [3a-f]

**Making skills and knowledge and understanding**
- Make rain gauges, using suitable materials. [4a-f]
- Use your rain gauges. Evaluate their success, durability, etc. [4f]

# R.E.

• Tell the Bible story of Noah and the Flood. Research and illustrate the story, and discuss its authenticity.

• Find out about and discuss why many people, through their religious lives, give thanks for the rain. For example, read prayers of thanks for rainy weather; talk about how this is often a feature of Harvest Festival services; organise your own 'Rain Assembly' for telling others about the essential role of rain in our lives.

• Investigate rain dances and other pagan celebrations and prayers designed to bring about rainfall or express thanks for it.

**Blueprints links**

**Distant Places:** Brazil copymasters 5–6; **Early Years Songs and Rhymes:** pages 34, 53; **Environmental Education Key Stage 1:** activities on water cycle, p. 149; **Geography Key Stage 1:** copymasters 101–4, 111; **Infant Geography Resource Bank:** section on weather and climate, copymasters 91–92, 102 (weather records, rainforests); **Poetry Book:** section on wind and storm, copymasters 33–6; **Religious Education Key Stage 1:** copymaster 77; **Topics 5–8:** topic on water with copymasters; **Writing 5–8:** copymaster 16.

# CHINA

## ENGLISH

- Find China on the globe and/or a world map
- Look at and discuss items made in China
- Read and tell stories about China
- Study the Chinese New Year and other festivals
- Investigate the 12 animals in the Chinese New Year cycle
- Write imaginary stories/poems linked with China
- Write factually about life in China, Chinese New Year, etc.
- Compile descriptive word lists for dragon, rooster, etc.
- Label classroom displays and write informative captions
- Record details of scientific investigations
- Write factual accounts of any school visits

## R.E.

- Study Chinese beliefs and philosophy
- Learn about the Christian story of the Creation, and scientific explanations as to the beginning of the world

## GEOGRAPHY

- Study China by looking at a world map or globe. Locate Great Britain
- Investigate the climates of China
- Learn about rice
- Compare with life in Great Britain
- Visit a Chinese supermarket

## MUSIC

- Learn about the pentatonic scale
- Listen to Chinese music
- Learn some songs about China. If possible, include Chinese songs
- Compose 'Chinese' music

## ART

- Experiment with writing/painting using a variety of paintbrushes
- Design and make table mats, cards, etc.
- Make coolie hats to wear
- Make lanterns to decorate the classroom
- Make dragon/lion masks
- Design and make a wall frieze
- Make silhouettes of animals in the Chinese New Year cycle
- Use clay to model Chinese New Year animals
- Study examples of Chinese art
- Learn about Chinese writing

## MATHEMATICS

- Study Chinese numbers 1–10
- Learn about symmetry

## ENVIRONMENTAL EDUCATION

- Talk about the importance of caring for our world
- Learn about endangered species with special reference to Chinese pandas

## HISTORY

- Learn about China's history in relation to government
- Draw sequence of events as a picture-story
- Talk about modern China
- Study the concept of 'fact' and 'fiction' and relate this to stories about China in the past
- Look at and discuss artefacts, pictures, and books about China

## P.E. (DANCE)

- Explore shape and movement in relation to the animals in the Chinese New Year
- Create a story in dance, using selected music

## DESIGN AND TECHNOLOGY

- Discuss a class Chinese meal or festival
- Design, plan, make and evaluate such items as greetings cards, table mats, etc.
- Use computer/DTP to write 'party' invitations, letters

## SCIENCE

- Learn about some Chinese inventions
- Talk about Chinese food
- Learn about basic foods of China
- Investigate Chinese pandas
- Study the origin of silk
- Learn about paper
- Cook a Chinese meal
- Investigate the natural resources of China

## IDEAS BANK

General starting points: Suggestions for programmes of study of core and foundation subjects relating to topic, and links with cross-curricular themes and R.E.

## STARTING POINTS

● Show the children a small diverse collection of arte-facts: discuss each one and let the children guess which country it came from. When each artefact has been discussed, reveal the 'Made In China' labels.

● Look at a globe and a world map to establish the location of China: discuss its position in relation to the British Isles and other prominent countries such as USA, India, Australia, and so on. Talk about the size of China and compare it with the British Isles.

● Ask children to bring in as many items as they can find with the words 'Made In China' on them, and arrange a display with other Chinese artefacts which may or may not be labelled (for example, fans, costumes, Chinese New Year serviettes, money bags, postage stamps, greetings cards, and so on).

● Try to arrange a visit to a Chinese supermarket, if there is one in the locality, so that the children can look at the range of different foods and wares on display.

● Arrange a display of Chinese pictures and photographs including some of temples and pagodas and animals depicting the cycle of years in the Chinese calendar.

● Try to arrange for a Chinese person to visit the school and talk to the children.

# ENGLISH

### Speaking and listening

● Begin this topic by looking at some items made in China and look at the globe or a map to find out where China is located. Look at the pictures, etc. on display and talk about them. [1a-d, 2a-b, 3a-b]

● Read or tell a selection of stories about China. Talk about these with the children and encourage discussion about Chinese customs, food, language and culture. [1a-d, 2a-b, 3a-b]

● Include tales of Chinese New Year and other festivals in your story telling. Tell the children about the twelve animals in the Chinese New Year cycle. Let them discover 'their' particular animal, provided they know when they were born. What is the animal of the current year? [1a-d, 2a-b, 3a-b]

### Reading

● After telling or reading appropriate stories and discussing them, let the children participate in re-reading part of a story or share the reading of a different poem or story. Make sure they are given help with the pronunciation of Chinese names etc. [1a-d, 2a, 2b, 2c, 3]

● Plan with the children the beginning of a story about, say, two of the animals in the Chinese New Year

cycle. Then either individually or in small groups, ask them to plan the middle and end of the story. Let them draw or write their story and finally read/tell it to the other children. [1a-d, 2a, 2b, 2c, 3]

### Writing

● Ask the children to draw/write imaginative stories about the topic of China. Chinese dragons and other animals should stimulate the imagination as well as stories about Festivals. [1a-c, 2a-e, 3a-b]

● Help the children to produce factual writing about life in China, the Chinese New Year, Chinese cooking, Chinese arts and traditions. [1a-c, 2a-e, 3a-b]

● Ask the children to make descriptive word lists for the dragon, the rooster, the snake and the other animals of the Chinese calendar. How many words can they produce for each animal? [1a-c, 2a-e, 3a-b]

● Make labels for class display, some giving information about a specific item, picture, etc. [1a-c, 2a-e, 3a-b]

(NOTE: Let the children copy a little Chinese writing. They will enjoy this activity but find it quite difficult. Tell children that the Chinese once used a thin brush and ink for writing, but today they increasingly use pencils and pens as we do.)

# SCIENCE

### Experimental and investigative science

All activities below provide opportunities for experimental and investigative science.

● Discuss Chinese food and cooking, and some Chinese inventions such as magnets, silk, paper, porcelain and china. Let the children look at examples of these items, including foodstuffs, at the appropriate time. [1a-c, 2a-c, 3a-f]

### Life processes and living things

● In class discussions, talk about other basic foods of China including rice, and the conditions under which it is grown. Let the children handle uncooked rice, examine the different kinds and learn what part of the plant it is. Cook a little rice and let the children observe changes during the cooking process, also how the clear water has become cloudy. Can they explain this? [1b, 2b, 3a-c, 4a-b, 5a-b]

• Talk about Chinese pandas and their dependence upon bamboo plants. Discuss the near extinction of this species and the breeding plans of certain zoos. Let the children draw and write what they know about pandas, and have pictures/books available for this piece of work. [1b, 4b, 5a-b]

**Materials and their properties**
• Show the children a piece of silk. Let them feel it and discuss how it was made/where it originated. Let them see pictures of moths, caterpillars and of course silkworms. Talk about the life-cycle of the moth and explain the basic origin of silk thread. Explain that silk is a natural material, though imitation silk is also manufactured. If possible, let the

children compare the two. Can they tell the difference? [1a, 1b, 1c, 1e]
• Talk about the Chinese invention of paper and let the children experiment in making their own recycled paper for use in Art. [1a, 1b, 1c, 1e, 2a]
• Let the children prepare the ingredients and help cook stir-fry, rice and/or chop suey for a Chinese meal. Bring a wok into school and explain its function as a traditional Chinese cooking utensil. Discuss its shape and the fact that the heat is evenly distributed across the cooking surface. Ensure that the children are carefully supervised while preparing the food and enlist an adult to take charge of the actual cooking/simmering over heat. Give the children adequate opportunity to examine what goes into the recipes and let everyone share in the food preparation. [1a, 1b, 2b]

# MATHEMATICS ▶

**Using and applying mathematics**
All activities below provide opportunities for using and applying mathematics.
• Let the children choose the materials and mathematics necessary for cooking. Encourage them to discuss their work, make predictions, solve any problems, etc. [1a, 2a, 2b, 2c, 2d, 4b]

**Number**
• Make an information sheet for each child showing Chinese numbers 1 – 10. If possible, include the pronunciation. Let the children enjoy making up Chinese sums, and let them mark each other's efforts if

they are old enough to cope with this. Alternatively, make a simple Chinese mathematics work sheet for each child. [1a, 1e, 2a]

**Shape, space and measures**
• Let the children splash coloured paints onto one half of a sheet of sugar paper, then fold the clean half onto the painted surface in order to obtain identical halves. Use the word 'symmetry' when talking about the children's work. After discussion, when the picture is dry, let them see if they can turn their painting into a dragon's face by painting on eyes, teeth, etc. Ask the children if their work is still symmetrical. [2c]

# DESIGN AND TECHNOLOGY ▶

**Design and technology capability**
• Tell the children that the Chinese love celebrations and they have many public festivals. Name the main ones, such as the Chinese New Year (Jan/Feb), the Dragon Boat Festival (May/June), and the Moon Festival (September). Tell the stories linked to the festivals and some of the exciting events that take place during festival time – the dragon and lion dances in the streets, lights and firecrackers, the giving of presents, and the preparation of special sweets and foods. Suggest that the class has its own Chinese party and begin to plan for it. Where will it be held? Will there be food? When will it be? If the party is linked to the Chinese New Year, plan for greetings cards, table mats, etc. [1a, 1b, 2a-c]

**Designing skills**
• Ask the children to design a greetings card, party invitation, table mat, fan, etc. Talk about these

and let the children decide whether they will all make the same design or attempt individual ones. Tell the children why red is the predominant colour for New Year cards, and show them how to write a New Year greeting (in Cantonese, this reads 'Kung Hei Fat(t) Choy' with a literal meaning of 'May you do well'). [3a-f]

**Making skills and knowledge and understanding**
• Let the children plan and make their chosen item(s) as described above. [4a, 4b, 4c, 4d, 4e, 5a-g]
• As a class, discuss the end products of the above activity. Is anything more required, for example, an invitation to the party for the head teacher, bowls, spoons, chopsticks, etc? Perhaps the school or teacher might offer to supply a packet of red paper serviettes, whilst the children bring their own dishes. Other items will, of course, be required – for example,

cordial to drink, and paper cups for convenience. Try to ensure that there are enough pairs of chopsticks to go around – children may be able to bring their own on party day, and these should be marked with the owner's name. [4f]

**Information technology**
- Using an appropriate word processing program, let children write their own letters home, explaining when their party will be held and that they will need a bowl, spoon, etc. on that day. Print these letters and send them home. [1a-c, 2a-c, 3a-c]

# ART

**Investigating and making**
- Let the children experiment with the use of paint-brushes and paints, attempting different strokes with the brush. If possible, show them some Chinese paintings before they attempt this task.
- Let the children design and make cards and table mats for their party. (Design and technology)
- Let the children make coolie hats to wear at the party, lanterns to decorate the room, a dragon and lion mask for the dances, etc.
- Plan a wall frieze and let all children make a contribution towards its creation. The frieze could depict the Chinese New Year story showing the twelve animals starting their race across the river, or a three-dimensional dragon, or any other relevant picture.
- Make a display of all the animals of the Chinese New Year cycle. Let the children cut outline silhouettes of the animals, preferably from gold or silver foil. Mount these on card and, if desired, add the message 'Kung hei fat choy' (meaning 'Happy New Year').

- Using clay or alternative modelling material, let the children make a model of their 'own animal', linking their birth date to the Chinese New Year.

**Knowledge and understanding**
- Let the children examine and discuss as many different forms of Chinese art as possible. Explain that Chinese people used to write with a brush and ink (calligraphy), and would begin to learn this technique at about six years of age. Nowadays, pens and pencils are most commonly used for writing, although calligraphy is also traditionally linked with painting – sometimes the Chinese will frame a piece of writing and use it as a picture. Try to obtain some prints of this style of painting to help the children understand this concept.
- Collect as many other artefacts as possible, in order to reinforce the Chinese art work with pictures, books, photographs and so on. Try also to display such items as rice bowls, chopsticks, screen prints, dress materials and designs on tins, boxes, etc.

# GEOGRAPHY

**Geographical skills and places**
- Find China on the globe and a world map. Also help the children to find Great Britain. Compare the size of the two countries: explain that China is the third largest country in the world, only Russia and Canada being bigger. Let the children find these two countries on the map or globe, and compare the land masses. [1c, 2, 3e, 3f, 4, 5a-d]
- Talk about the climate of the British Isles in relation to its position in the world and its size. Compare this with China and explain that. because the country is so big, it has many different climates – for example, cold-temperate, prairies and steppes, temperate, warm-temperate, tropical, conifer woods and deserts. Select two or three of these to illustrate China's differing climates, using examples that you know the children will more readily understand (such as deserts and tropics). State that where the climate is right, the Chinese people grow rice, tea, cotton and bananas as their main produce. Let the children record some simple facts about China. [1c, 2, 3e, 3f, 4, 5a-d]
- Explain to the children how rice has to be grown, introducing the word 'irrigation'. Describe the various stages of its growth, using pictures, books, school video-tape recordings by way of illustration. Ask the children to present their own account of the process, either by a

series of correctly sequenced and labelled pictures or by passages of writing, depending upon age and ability. [1c, 2, 3e, 3f, 4, 5a-d]
- Discuss how people work and live in Great Britain today. Let the children work in groups to see how many jobs of work they can identify in this country within, say, a five minute time period. Allow other short periods of time for consideration of such issues as what foods are grown in Britain (5 minutes), how many kinds of transport can be found (3 minutes), and so on. Compare these facts with what we know about China (for example, the main foods grown are rice, tea, etc; transport consists mainly of bicycles, trams and buses. Tell the children that China is a large oil-producing country which is expanding its industries, as we can see from the many goods available in this country. [1c, 2, 3e, 3f, 4, 5b, 5c, 5d]
- Discuss the use of natural materials in China, for example, the silk moth, making porcelain and the extraction of oil. [1c, 2, 3e, 3f, 4, 5b, 5c, 5d]

**Thematic study**
- Talk about rice and how the Chinese have changed their local environment through irrigation, in order to assist in its growth. [1c, 2, 3e, 3f, 4, 6a, 6b]

# HISTORY

**Areas of study (Key Elements 1-5)**

● In simple terms, explain to children that China is one country which has two governments – one on mainland China and the other on the island of Taiwan and groups of other tiny islands. Explain that this has been so since the late 1940s, at which time there was fighting over who should rule the country. As a result of that conflict, one group of people left to form a government in Taiwan while the others stayed in China. Tell the children also that for thousands of years before 1912, China was ruled by Emperors: after 1912, the country became a Republic and was governed without a royal family. Let the children outline the history of China by showing this sequence of events as a picture-story. [1, 3]

● As a class discuss modern China briefly, including a few facts which the children will understand and find interesting, for example:

- the Great Wall of China (the only man-made structure to be seen from outer space) which was built about 2,500 years ago
- the art of making china;
- the law by which Chinese families are 'fined' if they have more than one baby because already

there are more than a thousand million people living in China;

- the link between the ancient Chinese emperors and the dragon;
- the probability that such inventions as gunpowder and rockets originated in China;

and so on.

Let the children make their own fact sheet about China. [1, 2, 3]

● Make sure that the children understand that the history of China concerns people who really did live at that time, or who are living today – although some of the stories we read or hear may not always be strictly accurate. Point out, for example, that the Emperors were fact, but that the dragons were fiction. Differentiate between historical fact, for which we have genuine evidence, and fiction (or fantasy or fable) for which there is none. [1, 2, 3]

**Use of historical sources**

● Let the children look at pictures and books about China and examine all the artefacts on display. Use these for stimulating class discussions. What can the children discover by looking at pictures, artefacts and so on? [1, 2, 3]

# MUSIC

**Performing and composing**

● Tell children that Chinese music is based on a five note (or pentatonic scale), whereas European music uses an eight note scale. Most children will be able to sing 'doh-ray-me-fah-soh-lah-te-doh' in order to illustrate the latter scale: as they sing the notes, let the children count them on their fingers. Play a piece of Chinese music – does it sound different from the music we know?

● If possible, learn one or two Chinese songs which employ the pentatonic scale, and/or songs about China.

● Help the children to work in groups to make

Chinese-sounding music, perhaps using cymbals, chime bars, xylophones, etc., and possibly home-made instruments. Let the children record their music, so that other groups may listen and try to play it themselves from pictorial recording.

**Listening and appraising**

● Try to obtain some examples of Chinese music and play these to the children. Let them discuss the music, with its similarities to/differences from music in the Western world.

# P.E.

**Dance**

● In a series of lessons let the children explore shape and movement in relation to the twelve animals in the Chinese year.

● Let them work in groups to make up a story in

movement/dance about two or three chosen (by the teacher) animals, plus human(s). Each group should show its story to the rest of the class. Discuss each story, and give the children an opportunity for explanation if it was not clear from the performance.

101

# R.E.

- Tell the children simply about Chinese beliefs and thinking, and include the Chinese version of the creation of the Earth.
- Discuss the Christian story of how the Earth came into being and tell the children that there are many people who have other ideas, including scientists and their 'big bang' theories.

# ENVIRONMENTAL EDUCATION

- As a class, talk about the importance of caring for our Earth and not destroying it. Whatever we believe about how the Earth came into being, we must care for it now.
- Talk about endangered species, with specific reference to the Chinese pandas, and tell the children what China and other countries are doing to try to save them from extinction.

**Blueprints links**
**Art Key Stage 1:** copymaster 16 (willow pattern); **Art Resource Bank:** copymasters on Chinese Art, 16, 38, 51–2; **Festivals:** complete topic on Chinese New Year.

# CHOCOLATE

## ENGLISH

- Discuss chocolate words and thoughts
- Talk about textures
- Read poems and stories about chocolate
- Read chocolate recipes
- Set up a 'chocolate' reading corner
- Read product labels
- Discuss published stories about chocolate
- Write a recipe book
- Write poems and stories about chocolate
- Write captions for pictures
- Compose new chocolate names
- Write a chocolate book
- Write advertising slogans

## HISTORY

- Research the origins of the chocolate industry

## HEALTH EDUCATION

- Consider the nutritional value of chocolate

## ECONOMIC AND INDUSTRIAL UNDERSTANDING

- Run a classroom chocolate shop or business

## DESIGN AND TECHNOLOGY

- Store and retrieve chocolate data on a computer database

**CHOCOLATE**

## GEOGRAPHY

- Research the environment of the Cacao plant
- Do a sub-topic on Mexico
- Investigate the chocolate industry
- Investigate the weather conditions needed for producing chocolate

## MATHEMATICS

- Collect data on chocolate and record in appropriate ways
- Do calorie calculations
- Run a chocolate shop

## ART

- Paint advertisements
- Make collages/montages

## SCIENCE

- Discuss qualities of chocolate
- Taste different types of chocolate
- Pose and test questions about chocolate
- Do 'fair tests' on chocolate
- Investigate textures
- Research the origins of chocolate
- Find out about the cacao plant
- Discuss chocolate as a food source
- Find out about calories in chocolate
- Heat and cool chocolate
- Cook chocolate
- Research ingredients in chocolate
- Experiment with the properties of chocolate

**IDEAS BANK**

General starting points: Suggestions for programmes of study of core and foundation subjects relating to topic, and links with cross-curricular themes and R.E.

**STARTING POINTS**

- Eat chocolate: sample various types.

- Start with a tin of cocoa powder and begin an investigation of the origins of cocoa/chocolate.
- Make a collection of pictures (from magazines, food labels, etc.) of all the edible things you can find that contain chocolate or cocoa.
- Read the story of 'Charlie and The Chocolate Factory' by Roald Dahl.

# SCIENCE ▶

**Experimental and investigative science**

All activities below provide opportunities for experimental and investigative science.

- Take a good look at chocolate. Discuss its colour texture and appearance. [2a, 2b, 3a, 3c, 3f]
- Provide small samples of chocolate in various colours (milk chocolate, plain chocolate, white chocolate) for the children to taste and discuss differences in flavour. Record preferences and reasons for these. [1a-c, 2a-c, 3a-f]
- Pose questions for testing, for example, what would happen if ... chocolate was heated or cooled (Link with Materials and their properties). [1a-c, 2a-c, 3a-f]
- Discuss and carry out the need for a fair test on predictions and investigations, for example, the need to use chocolate of the same variety when heating or cooling it. (Link with Materials and their properties.) [1a-c, 2a-c, 3a-f]
- Observe and take chocolates of different textures such as solid block chocolate, flake chocolate, chocolate with air bubbles in it, and so on. Decide whether the texture affects taste and suggest preferences. Do 'blind testing', i.e. blindfold children and ask them to describe the texture of the chocolate they are tasting. [1a-c, 2a-c, 3a-f]

**Life processes and living things**

- Research the origins of the ingredients of chocolate; in particular find out about the cacao plant, from which chocolate and cocoa come. Find out the parts this plant has, and from which parts chocolate derives its key ingredients [1a, 3b, 3c]
- Find out how and where the cocoa plant grows (relate to geography activities) and conditions necessary to sustain its growth, i.e. light, temperature, warmth, nourishment, etc. [1a, 3a, 5b]
- Discuss the place of chocolate as a food source, i.e. as a supplier of energy to the human body; perhaps

relating this to other work on the topics of energy and food. [1b, 2c]

- Following on from the above, consider the value of chocolate as a food source, i.e. is it a 'good' or 'bad' food? Relate to calorific content of food, the need for a balanced diet and classification of food energy sources (simple and complex carbohydrates, proteins, fats). [2c]
- Read chocolate commodity packaging to find out how many calories there are in a specified amount of chocolate, or products containing chocolate. Compare with calories in other types of food of the same size and weight. Find out how many calories human beings need to help them stay alive and active. (Relate to mathematics activities.) [1b, 2c]

**Materials and their properties**

- Investigate what happens to chocolate when it is heated. Melt some chocolate at various temperatures. [2b]
- Investigate whether melting is a permanent change. Remove chocolate from heat source and observe what happens. [2b]
- Find out what if anything happens when chocolate is made colder rather than heated. Keep some in a refrigerator for a period of time; freeze some. [2b]
- Cook chocolate: try out a variety of recipes involving the heating and cooling of chocolate. Discuss how changes in the substance are essential for producing the desired product. [1a, 2b]
- Find out more about other ingredients that are necessary (apart from the seed of the cacao plant) to make chocolate. Discuss the properties of these and research the heating (roasting) and cooling processes necessary to make the product. [1a, 2a-b]
- Experiment with the properties of cocoa powder; mix with liquid, heat and observe results. Cool the end product and observe results. [1a, 2a-b]

# GEOGRAPHY ▶

**Geographical skills and places**
- Find out more about the Mexican plant from which cocoa and chocolate derive – *Theobroma Cacao*. Research the nature of the places where this originated and grows. [1c, 2, 3a, 3e, 3f, 4, 5a-d]
- Use this topic as an opportunity to develop related work, or perhaps a future topic on the country of Mexico; its landscape, people, ways of life and economy. [1c, 2, 3a, 3e, 3f, 4, 5a-d]
- Research the present day chocolate industry – the locations of this, people employed in it, the tasks they do, transport and communication between importing/exporting countries etc. [1c, 2, 3e, 3f, 4, 5c, 5d]
- Find out about weather conditions necessary for the growth of the cacao plant. Discuss why we do not grow it in the UK. Compare climate in places where it is grown to our own. [1c, 2, 3e, 3f, 4, 5a-d]
- Help children to appreciate the cacao's need for soil and water, and that these are part of the natural environment of places where the plant thrives. [4, 5b, 5c]

# HISTORY ▶

**Areas of study (Key elements 1a-b, 2b, 4a-b, 5a)**
- Read about and research the historic origins of chocolate as a consumer product and major industry.

Find out about the role of the Spanish in first bringing cocoa from central America to Europe. [1a-b, 3]

# MATHEMATICS ▶

**Using and applying mathematics**
All activities provide opportunities for using and applying mathematics.

**Number**
- Do calculations based on calorie counts, for example, of the number of calories consumed in a given number of chocolates or chocolate bars. [1a-f, 2a, 2b]
- Do calculations which compare the calories consumed in a certain amount of chocolate with those consumed in the same weight of other varieties of foodstuffs. [1a-f, 2a, 2b, 3c, 3d, 3e, 4a-d, 5a-b]
- Do sums about the price of chocolate and chocolate products. Organise a classroom 'chocolate shop' for the children to buy and sell goods. [1a, 1c, 1e, 2a-c, 3b, 3d, 4a, 4b]

**Classifying, representing and interpreting data**
- Collect data from the class or a school survey on chocolate colour preferences (plain, milk, white); chocolate texture preferences (solid, flake, with air holes) and chocolate products (cake, assorted bars, soft-centred sweets, etc.) Collate this data in appropriate ways, and construct and interpret related graphs and other statistical diagrams. [5a-b]
- Transfer the above data to appropriate computer databases and retrieve information. [5b]

# DESIGN AND TECHNOLOGY ▶

**Information technology capability**
- Use a computer to store and retrieve data about chocolate and chocolate products (relate to mathematics activities). Retrieve information when required. [1b, 2b, 2c]

# ENGLISH ▶

## Speaking and listening

- Ask the children to close their eyes and think about chocolate and to say words that come into their minds. Discuss 'chocolate thoughts'. [1a-d, 2a-b, 3a-b]
- Make a list of 'chocolate words' by discussing the vocabulary that best describes the substance as a result of exploring chocolate through all the senses (feel, smell, sight, taste, touch). [1a, 1b, 1c, 2a-b, 3a-b]
- Talk about different textures of chocolate, reminding children of its various forms (flaky, solid, aerated, soft, liquid, etc.) [1a, 1b, 1c, 2a-b, 3a-b]
- Read aloud any stories, poems and rhymes you can find about chocolate, such as 'Charlie and The Chocolate Factory'. Discuss. [1a, 1b, 1c, 2a-b, 3a-b]

## Reading

- Encourage the children to read recipes which require the use of chocolate or cocoa as a main ingredient. [1b, 1c, 2a-d]
- Ask the children to read aloud their own poems and stories about chocolate for other children to listen to and discuss. [1a, 1c, 2a, 2c, 3]
- Set up a display of books about chocolate (fiction, recipe books, non-fiction and reference material) for the children to consult as required. [1b, 1c, 2a-d, 3]
- Collect labels from chocolate products. Display these as reading material for the children to access information about names of products, weight, content, etc. [1b, 1c, 2a-d, 3]
- Discuss stories that have been read on the topic, using previous reading experience and knowledge about chocolate to show an appreciation of meaning beyond the literal. [1a-c, 2a-d, 3]

## Writing

- Write your own class recipe book containing a range of recipes with chocolate as a central ingredient. [1a-c, 2a-e, 3a-b]
- Write descriptive poems and other forms of writing about chocolate, utilising words thought of in class discussions about exploration of chocolate using all the senses. [1a-c, 2a-e, 3a-b]
- Cut out pictures of chocolate products from magazines. Display these as discussion material and ask children to write simple captions to describe them. [1a-c, 2a-e, 3a-b]
- Paint pictures of imaginary chocolate products. Let the children think up suitable names and write them alongside the pictures. [1a-c, 2a-e, 3b]
- Write up the results of scientific investigations into the world of chocolate, and non-fiction accounts deriving from research into scientific, historical and geographical aspects of the topic. [1a-c, 2a-e, 3a-b]
- Write imaginative stories related to chocolate. Let the children think of their own plots or titles or provide suggestions such as 'The Cacao Plant That Came To Life', 'The Chocolate Sea', 'Raining Chocolate', etc. [1a-c, 2a-e, 3a-b]
- Compose a 'Chocolate' book, a class scrapbook containing children's own stories and poems on the subject, recipes, facts about chocolate, pictures, etc. [1a-c, 2a-e, 3a-b]
- Write slogans for chocolate advertisements (relate to art activities). [1a-c, 2a-e, 3a-b]

# ECONOMIC AND INDUSTRIAL UNDERSTANDING ▶

- Design and organise a classroom chocolate shop or business – selling imaginary products for mathematical and business design experience, or real products for fund raising.

# ART ▶

## Investigating and making

- Design and paint posters of advertisements for chocolate and chocolate products. Compose and add suitable slogans.
- Make collages/montages with labels from chocolate products.

# HEALTH EDUCATION

● Consider the role of chocolate in our diet (relate to science activities) – its value as a food source, and also the need to take care not to eat too much of it.

**Blueprints links**
**Christmas Key Stage 1:** topic on Christmas food;
**Christmas Art and Craft:** chocolate recipes.

# PICTURES

## ENGLISH

- Discuss pictures on display
- Tell/write an imaginary picture story
- Study the concept of imaginary pictures
- Write and tell imaginary stories/poems relating to pictures
- Read stories and poems aloud
- Write labels for displays
- Write factually about school visit(s) and other matters relating to the topic
- Record details of scientific investigations

## ART

- Make a wide variety of pictures
- Design a large frieze picture
- Study a wide range of paintings, including some by well-known artists
- Visit a local park or similar to draw something of interest

## P.E. (DANCE)

- Create a simple story in dance

## MUSIC

- Discuss music, pictures and imagination
- Create a dance sequence after listening to selected descriptive music

**PICTURES**

## GEOGRAPHY

- Look at pictures of local area
- Look at pictures of other localities
- Obtain children's views about aesthetic features of local area

## MATHEMATICS

- Plan and measure for a class 'art gallery'
- Learn about fractions
- Study shapes in painting
- Investigate symmetry
- Represent data pictorially and on a database

## HISTORY

- Draw or paint a sequence of pictures
- Study selected pictures about the past, including some depicting 'real' events in history
- Find out what can be deduced from pictures of the past
- Investigate the making of cartoon films

## DESIGN AND TECHNOLOGY

- Identify needs for a picture display
- Design, plan, make and evaluate end results
- Use computer drawing or painting programs

## SCIENCE

- Investigate materials used in picture making
- Learn about natural and human-made materials
- Investigate origins of some natural materials
- Study paper and its production
- Discuss recycling

**IDEAS BANK**
General starting points: Suggestions for programmes of study of core and foundation subjects relating to topic, and links with cross-curricular themes and R.E.

**STARTING POINTS**
● Arrange a surprise display of pictures by well-known artists. Calendars, magazines, the local library, markets and so on are good sources for inexpensive prints. Try to collect a variety of contrasting pictures rather than a gallery of country scenes!

● Encourage children to bring into school a picture of their own choice, and explain their reasons for choosing it. Discuss various aspects of all pictures during the period of the topic.
● Arrange a visit to a local art gallery so that children can experience the viewing of selected works of art in this setting. This outing could be planned as part of a day excursion, with children also visiting a local park or garden where they could draw their own pictures of views, plants, flowers, trees and so on.

# ENGLISH ▶

**Speaking and listening**
● Look at the pictures on display and discuss these over a period of time. Let children choose their favourite picture and give reasons for their choice. [1a-d, 2a-b, 3a-b]
● Tell the children to work in pairs or small groups and plan an imaginary story about a picture of their choice. Initially, some guidance may be necessary – for example, suggest that the children pretend that a person(s) or animal(s) in the picture comes to life, and tell the story of what happens. When they are ready, let the children tell their stories to the rest of the class. [1a-d, 2a-b, 3a-b]

**Reading**
● Talk to the children about imaginary pictures of the mind. Read a selection of poems and stories over a period of time and encourage the children to describe their individual imaginary pictures about a character or event. [1a, 1c, 1d, 2a, 2b, 2c, 3]

● Begin a story concerning a picture of some kind, perhaps with a title like 'The Hidden Picture' or 'The Picture That Moved'. Ask children to continue the story and complete it. Let them read or tell their stories to the rest of the class. [1a, 1c, 1d, 2a, 2b, 2c, 3]

**Writing**
● Let children write imaginary stories about pictures, for example, 'The Stolen Picture', 'Picture Magic', 'When The Picture Came To Life', etc. [1a-c, 2a-e, 3a-e]
● Make informative labels about pictures on display. [1a-c, 2a-e, 3a-e]
● Write a factual account of any school visit to observe or draw pictures. [1a-c, 2a-e, 3a-e]
● Write about changes observed in pictures from other times. [1a-c, 2a-e, 3a-e]
● Record details of investigations into natural materials conducted as part of science activities. [1a-c, 2a-e, 3a-e]

# SCIENCE ▶

**Experimental and investigative science**
All activities marked with an asterisk below provide opportunities for experimental and investigative science.

**Materials and their properties**
● *Discuss the various materials used in the making of pictures. Talk about natural and human-made materials, and how/where they are used. [1a-e, 2a-b]
● *Look at the origins of natural materials such as chalk, charcoal, canvas, dyes, and wood. Talk about

people-made materials and how difficult it sometimes is to tell natural materials from those made by people, for example, picture frames. [1a-e, 2a-b]
● Encourage children to bring in some articles: talk about what they are made of, and arrange a display of natural materials and people-made materials. [1a-e, 2a-b]
● *Talk to the children about paper, its origins and use in school. Discuss recycling, and let the children experiment in making their own recycled paper for use in art work. [1a-e, 2a]

109

# MATHEMATICS

**Using and applying mathematics**
All activities below provide opportunities for using and applying mathematics.

**Number**
- Discuss halves, quarters and thirds, and indicate these when talking about the content of pictures. [2c]
- Let the children construct graphs or other diagrams to show, for example, different categories of pictures, favourite pictures and so on. [1a, 1e]

**Shape, space and measures**
- Encourage children to select the materials and mathematics necessary for measuring and planning their 'art gallery'. Let them discuss their work with others and encourage them to resolve any related problems. [4a-b]
- Show the children prints of pictures by Piet Mondrian. Discuss these and the shapes used. Encourage children to use correct mathematical terms when describing two-dimensional shapes and three-dimensional objects. Give children the opportunity to create their own abstract pictures. [2a-c]
- Talk about common picture shapes. [2a-c]
- Look at some pictures with identical halves (for example, a butterfly or a spider) and introduce the concept of symmetry. [2c]

# DESIGN AND TECHNOLOGY

**Design and technology capability**
- With the class, evaluate the classroom and/or the school in relation to pictures: talk about pictorial displays in the school and how effective they are. Encourage the children to express their views. [1a, 1b, 2c]
- Let the children decide where pictures might be displayed to advantage. [1a, 1b, 2c]

**Designing skills**
- Ask children to work individually or in groups to make a special display picture or wall frieze. Encourage discussion and sketches or drawings before a final design is chosen. Make sure that the children have considered the size of picture in relation to the space available. Select the materials and techniques to be used. [3a-f]

**Making skills and knowledge and understanding**
- Let the children make their planned picture using chosen materials. [4a-e, 5a-g]
- Discuss the pictures when they are completed, 'framed' and displayed. [4f]
- Let the children evaluate their own work and overall results. [4f]

**Information technology**
- If the facilities are available, and such activities are within the ability range of the children, let them use appropriate computer drawing or painting programs to make on-screen pictures. Print them, using a colour printer, if possible. If the school has access to a PC with an SVGA or a VGA card, consider introducing the children to fractal graphics programs – a little experimentation can generate some colourful and kaleidoscopic effects on the monitor screen. [1a-c, 3a-c]

# ART

**Investigating and making**
- Use as wide a range of materials and techniques as possible for making pictures in art work.
- Let the children create a special picture of their choice, real or imaginary, to be 'framed' and hung when completed.
- Let the children work together to create other artwork, as suggested in Design and Technology, including a large frieze picture. Discuss all the art work as a class when it has been completed.

**Knowledge and understanding**
- Collect as wide a variety of pictures as possible from both past and present. Discuss these and also the differences between photographs and paintings, etc.
- Let the children talk at length about one or two pictures at a time, for example, materials used, techniques adopted, the composition of the picture, its theme, mood, and so on.
- Let the class discuss and evaluate their own displays of pictures.

# GEOGRAPHY

**Geographical skills and places**
● Show the children photographs and/or pictures of any interesting features of the local area. Talk about these, and find out whether the children can suggest other places worth painting or photographing. [3a,3f]
● Compare pictures from other localities with those already discussed, for example, the different land-scapes. Ask the children to bring in their own selection of examples both from this country and abroad. [3f, 4, 5a-d, 6a]
● Let the children express their own views about the local environment. Are there features worth making pictures of? What would they choose as a subject to paint, if at all? [6a-c]

# HISTORY

**Areas of study (Key Elements 1-5)**
● Ask the children to draw pictures in a correct sequence to illustrate a story about the past. This can be, for example, the story of their own lives thus far – birth, toddler, nursery, school, etc. – or a story told by the teacher. [1a, 1b, 2, 3]
● Discuss other selected pictures and/or photographs showing life in the past. [1a, 1b, 2, 3]
● Explain to the children the principles by which cartoon films – thousands of coloured pictures which can be manipulated in such a way that the characters depicted within them appear to move – are created. The children may like to attempt to animate a series of draw-ings of their own, using the same principles. Go on, perhaps, to explain how live action films are made. [3]

**Interpretations of history**
● Choose one or two pictures showing 'real' events in history, and tell the stories behind them – exam-ples might include Guy Fawkes, Scott of the Antarc-tic, the evacuation of children in World War II, the Spanish Armada, Apollo XI and the first man on the moon, etc. Talk about true and/or fictional stories. [2, 3]

**Use of historical sources**
● Let the children study some of the pictures of past events and people, and tell or write what can be learned from such pictures. [2, 3]

# MUSIC

**Listening and appraising**
● Discuss with the class the similarity or connec-tion between pictures and music – music can also 'paint' a picture (in one's mind). Play extracts from some descriptive music such as Manuel de Falla's 'Ritual Fire Dance', Handel's 'Water Music', Beethoven's 'Pastoral Symphony', Saint Saens' 'Carni-val Of The Animals', Honegger's 'Pacific 231' (a classic representation in music of a steam locomotive), Smetana's 'Ma Vlast', Strauss's 'Thunder and Light-ning Polka', Grieg's 'In The Hall Of The Mountain King', perhaps even John Williams's film music for 'Jaws', and so on.
● Talk about the 'pictures' that such pieces of music create. Let the children describe their own imaginative pictures after listening to some of them. Discuss the rhythms of the music, its dynamics and pace, etc.
● Use some of this music for movement and dance. Encourage the children to interpret their mental 'pictures' in dance.

# P.E.

**Dance**
● Use music relating to the topic to enable children to explore mood, rhythm, etc.
● Let the children work in groups to create a simple story to one piece of music. Ask them to show their story (musical pictures) to the rest of the class.

**Blueprints links**
**Art Key Stage 1:** a complete resource on making pictures; **Art Resource Bank:** the whole book is a rich photocopiable resource of pictures and art styles; **History Key Stage 1:** copymasters 1–3 (family portraits); **Poetry Book:** section on portraits, copy-masters 45–8; **Religious Education Key Stage 1:** 1, 12: **Writing Book:** copymaster 61.